Technology and Military Doctrine
Essays on a Challenging Relationship

I. B. HOLLEY JR.
Major General, USAF, Retired

Air University Press
Maxwell Air Force Base, Alabama

August 2004

Disclaimer

Opinions, conclusions, and recommendations expressed or implied within are solely those of the editor and do not necessarily represent the views of Air University, the United States Air Force, the Department of Defense, or any other US government agency.

Air University Press
131 West Shumacher Avenue
Maxwell AFB AL 36112-6615

Published by Books Express Publishing
Copyright © Books Express, 2011
ISBN 978-1-78039-969-0

Books Express publications are available from all good retail and online booksellers. For publishing proposals and direct ordering please contact us at: info@books-express.com

Doctrinal inadequacy is no less often the cause of defeat, or of unnecessary reverses, than is technological backwardness.

—Colin S. Gray

THIS PAGE INTENTIONALLY LEFT BLANK

Contents

Illustrations

Tables

About the Author

Professor I. B. Holley Jr. is an emeritus member of the Department of History, Duke University, Durham, North Carolina, where he has served since 1947. He taught US social and intellectual history with special interest in military history and the history of technology. Among his better known writings are *Ideas and Weapons: Exploitation of the Aerial Weapon by the United States in World War I; A Study in the Relationship of Technological Advance, Military Doctrine, and the Development of Weapons* (Yale University Press, 1953), reprinted by Archon Books (1971) and the Government Printing Office (1983 and 1997); *Buying Aircraft: Air Materiel Procurement for the Army Air Forces,* a volume in the Official History of the US Army in World War II (1964); and a biography, *General John M. Palmer: Citizen Soldiers and the Army of Democracy,* published by Greenwood Press in 1982. His specialty is the field of military doctrine. Although retired, Professor Holley still teaches undergraduate and graduate students.

Professor Holley enlisted in the Army Air Forces in World War II, served as an aerial gunner instructor, and returned to private life after five years of active duty. He retired in February 1981 as a major general in the Air Force after nearly 40 years as a reservist. In his final duty assignment he served as assistant to the commander of Air University, Maxwell Air Force Base, Montgomery, Alabama.

Professor Holley was for 10 years chairman of the Advisory Committee on History (appointed by the secretary of the Air Force) and has been a member of the National Aeronautics and

Space Administration's history advisory committee. He has been a trustee of the American Military Institute and is currently a member of the advisory boards of *Air Power History*, the *Air and Space Power Journal*, and the *Air Force Journal of Logistics*. In 1974 he gave the Harmon Memorial Lecture at the Air Force Academy, "An Enduring Challenge: The Problem of Air Force Doctrine." During the academic year 1974–75, he was visiting professor of military history at the United States Military Academy, West Point, New York; in 1978–79 he held a similar appointment at the National Defense University in Washington, D.C. Professor Holley has frequently lectured at the Air War College, the Army War College, the Army Command and General Staff College, and the Pentagon. He also has taught at the Marine Corps University at Quantico, Virginia, and at the Militärhögskolan, the Military Staff College, in Sweden. He has been invited to give papers in Israel, Germany, and England.

Professor Holley received a Bachelor of Arts degree from Amherst College (1940) and a Master of Arts (1942) and Doctor of Philosophy (1947) from Yale University where he received the Tew Prize as the outstanding scholar in history in 1941 and the Townshend Prize for the best dissertation in 1947. He received Social Science Research Council Fellowships in 1955 and 1961 and was a Smithsonian Institution Fellow in 1968. He is an Associate Fellow of the American Institute of Aeronautics and Astronautics. In 1975 he received the Outstanding Civilian Service medal from the US Army, and in 1979 he received the Exceptional Civilian Service medal from the US Air Force, which also awarded him the Distinguished Service Medal and the Legion of Merit.

Acknowledgements

The author wishes to thank the Publication Review Board of the Air University Press for selecting this manuscript for publication. I extend my sincere thanks to Thomas Lobenstein and Carolyn McCormack for their conscientious editorial assistance and to Dr. Jim Titus who first suggested the idea of publishing an anthology of my doctrinal writings.

THIS PAGE INTENTIONALLY LEFT BLANK

Introduction

My interest in Air Force doctrine was first aroused when I was a sergeant serving as an aerial gunnery instructor in early 1943. When the operational research people revealed that what we were teaching was faulty, I came to realize that the Air Force system for developing doctrine was flawed. The problem continued to interest me and later, after I was commissioned and serving on the faculty of the Industrial College of the Armed Forces, I wrote my book *Ideas and Weapons*[1] using the experience of the air arm to expound the need for a more systematic procedure for developing doctrine. Because the doctrinal materials I had gathered on World War II were still highly classified, I reverted to World War I to put across my thesis without violating security. My real concern was to contribute to the soon to be established US Air Force in the search for a more effective means of formulating doctrine.

The essays that follow reflect how my ideas developed over the 30-odd years of my Air Force career. Inevitably there are some overlaps and repetitions given the origin of these essays as articles and lectures spread over many years. The main themes are evident. I repeatedly made the case for the importance of doctrine and the need to perfect the technological advances in equipment. I was concerned to see that doctrine was continually perfected in peacetime and not just in wartime when the pressure of enemy performance provides a powerful incentive to do this. Another theme repeatedly stated was the need for officers suitably educated to see the importance of doctrine and realize that doctrine is literally "everybody's business" and not just the concern of a handful of individuals assigned to the formal task of compiling doctrinal manuals. These people are important, but they cannot perform effectively if officers throughout the service fail to write after-action reports summarizing their valuable experiences, not just in air operations but in all aspects of the air arm activities, procurement, personnel administration, logistics, and legislative liaison. One can easily make the case that improving the ability of the Air Force to cope with Congress is just as important as suggesting the best possible doctrine for aerial combat. One can't just assume that every newly promoted flag officer will instinctively understand the best way of testifying on Capitol Hill.

Much of the doctrinal problem within the Air Force stems from the professional education of officers. Unless they are rigorously educated to undertake the objective analysis of recorded historical experience, all the most carefully edited doctrinal manuals will avail little. One of my insistent themes is the need to make doctrinal manuals not only more readable but more memorable. To this end several of the following essays are addressed to those who are assigned as doctrinal writers.

Notes

1. I. B. Holley Jr., *Ideas and Weapons: Exploitation of the Aerial Weapon by the United States during World War I; A Study in the Relationship of Technology Advance, Military Doctrine, and the Development of Weapons* (Hamden, Conn.: Archon Books, 1971).

Essay 1

The Role of Doctrine*

The armed forces of a nation are maintained principally to provide the means by which external threats can be countered.
These forces function in two ways: they may resist attack by the
direct application of force or they may seek to deter would-be ag-
gressors from attacking by maintaining a military potential sufficiently powerful to dissuade them from initiating such a move.
To prevail in a resort to force or to ensure the credibility of the
deterrence, the armed forces of a nation must have a sufficient
number of troops at an appropriate level of training armed with
weapons and equipment not inferior to those of a potential enemy.
But large numbers and superior weapons—and all that the existence of these assets connotes in the way of political support to
provide the necessary funds and industrial support—including
research, development, and logistics—to provide weapons with a
suitable margin of superiority—are not enough to ensure success in a resort to arms. Unless the armed forces are guided by
appropriate doctrines, greater numbers and superior weapons
are no guarantee of victory.

What, then, is doctrine? Reduced to its simplest terms, doctrine is what is officially approved to be taught—whether in a
service school or an operational unit engaged in training—
about what methods to use to carry out a military objective.
While doctrine is most commonly thought of as relating to
military action, the term is not limited to tactical applications.
There can, and should, be doctrine guiding personnel actions,
the acquisition process, logistical operations, purchasing, and
other support tasks.

For the most part, doctrine is derived from past experience;
it reflects an official recognition of what has usually worked

---

*This brief statement was originally drafted as a suggestion for the chief of staff of
the Air Force to use as an introduction to a forthcoming revision of Air Force Manual
1-1, *Air Force Basic Doctrine*. It appeared in the *Air Force Journal of Logistics*, Winter
1986, in slightly revised form to introduce an issue of the journal devoted to the newly
promulgated combat support doctrine.

best from observation of numerous trials. These may be reports of actual combat operations, or they may be limited to tests, exercises, and maneuvers. Only when necessary will doctrine consist of extrapolations beyond actual experience of some sort, for example, in the use of nuclear weapons where the nature of the weapon normally precludes the gathering of experience in any but the most limited sense.

Doctrine, as officially promulgated, has two main purposes. First, it provides guidance to decision makers and those who develop plans and policies, offering suggestions about how to proceed in a given situation on the basis of a body of past experience in similar contexts distilled down to concise and readily accessible doctrinal statements. Second, formal doctrines provide common bases of thought and common ways of handling problems, tactical or otherwise, which may arise. In the absence of communication with superiors, subordinates who are guided by doctrine in shaping a course of action will have a greater probability of conforming to the larger operation than if they were to act without knowledge of the doctrinal guidelines.

The term *guideline* is appropriate, for doctrine lays out a suggested course but is not mandatory. In the words of the official definition in Joint Chiefs of Staff Publication 1 (JCS Pub 1), *The Dictionary of US Military Terms for Joint Usage*, doctrine is "authoritative but requires judgment in application." An earlier version of Pub 1 put it even better, observing that doctrines "indicate and guide but do not bind in practice."

To understand *what doctrine is not* is no less important than knowing what it is. *Doctrine* is not to be confused with *strategy*. At its highest level, *grand strategy*, the latter term is virtually synonymous with national policy and embraces all the means used by a nation to carry out its policies—diplomatic, economic, social, or military.

Military strategy involves the selection of objectives and courses of action, the choice of targets, and the selection of forces to be employed. Military strategy is concerned with the ends sought and the means to attain those ends. Doctrine, by contrast, has nothing to say about the ends sought, as these can be ephemeral, reflecting the ebb and flow of policy.

2

Doctrine is, however, related to *means*. If strategy is concerned with *what* is to be done, doctrine involves *how* it is to be carried out. Where the defection of an ally or some other sudden turn of events may require an abrupt change in strategy, doctrine responds to a different set of variables. One such is the introduction of a novel and highly effective weapon by the enemy, requiring a recasting of doctrine when the experience of the past no longer offers an adequate guide for coping.

Manifestly, then, it becomes a matter of crucial importance to be sure that doctrine, as officially promulgated, is kept abreast of the times. Doctrine must be periodically revised to respond to advances in technology and other variables. This is a formidable task. In organizations as large as the armed forces, literally tens of thousands of individuals may be involved in the process of learning from experience and passing the word up to those in authority. While certain members of the staff at headquarters may be charged with responsibility for developing revised doctrines, the individuals involved cannot effectively carry out their duties without the cooperation of many others in the operating echelons who alone can provide the detailed feedback required to make sound adjustments and modifications to existing doctrine and, where necessary, to *generate new doctrine in hitherto untouched areas.*

Because those charged with the formulation of doctrine depend upon feedback from observers in the operating echelons—feedback which is both timely and cast in a form to maximize its usefulness—all potential contributors who upgrade doctrine should understand the role they, as individuals, are asked to play. By seeing his or her part in the larger whole, the individual officer or enlisted person will be better equipped and more inclined to exercise that initiative which differentiates the true professional from the mere timeserver.

3

THIS PAGE INTENTIONALLY LEFT BLANK

Essay 2

The Doctrinal Process: Some Suggested Steps[*]

Thoughtful observers of military institutions have often remarked that tactical doctrine normally has lagged far behind the hither edge of technological advance. All too often, new devices are perfected, put into production, and even issued to the troops in quantity only to languish there, marginally exploited, far below the potential utility inherent in the equipment. This is the challenge confronting all of us who would study the problem of military doctrine: Why does tactical doctrine fall so far behind the latent capabilities of technological innovations?

Recently, while checking a point in the *Encyclopedia Britannica,* I stumbled upon this answer to our question:

> The evolution of tactics is continuous. Formalism and traditionalism in most armies resist the evolution of tactics. The evolution goes on in spite of the professional soldier, instead of with his aid and encouragement. In all armies there are individuals who are far in advance of the practice of their times, whom history later proves correct. Those individuals rarely reach high place in armies. When they do, the stupendous conquests of Napoleon or the equally incredible conquests of modern Germany take place. Napoleon had no weapons better than his adversaries. He merely took advantage of their possibilities. . . . The secret of tactical success is to be found in a flexible intelligence of the higher military leaders. Unfortunately, most armies are so organized as to repress anything other than the traditional and habitual, and great nations fall to ruin on account of the ignorance and formalism of their generals.[1]

That jibe at the generals is not, as one might suspect, the work of some cloistered scholar who never had to face the burdens and the bite of command. It was written by a brigadier general in the US Army. Regrettably, his diagnosis offers but limited scope for remedial action. Even if we were certain what the author

*This essay was originally presented at a symposium sponsored by the US Army Command and General Staff College at Fort Leavenworth, Kansas, in March 1978. It was subsequently published in *Military Review* 59 (April 1979).

meant by a "flexible intelligence," it is difficult to perceive just what institutional arrangements might be contrived to overcome the defect.

In this essay I present a somewhat different interpretation of why doctrine so often seems to lag behind technology, one that offers greater scope for corrective action. My guiding text is drawn from Adm Alfred Thayer Mahan's *The Influence of Sea Power Upon History, 1660–1783.* In one highly perceptive passage, the admiral provides us with a sweeping overview of the whole process of doctrinal development:

> The unresting progress of mankind causes continual change in weapons; and with that must come a continual change in the manner of fighting. . . . The seaman who carefully studies the causes of success or failure . . . will observe that changes in tactics have not only taken place after changes in weapons, which is necessarily the case, but that the interval between such changes has been unduly long. This doubtless arises from the fact that an improvement in weapons is due to the energy of one or two men, while changes in tactics have to overcome the inertia of a conservative class; but it is a great evil. It can be remedied only by a candid recognition of each change by careful study of the powers and limitations of the new . . . weapon, and by a consequent adaptation of the method of using it to the qualities it possesses, which will constitute its tactics. History shows it is vain to hope that military men generally will be at pains to do this, but that the one who does will go into battle with a great advantage—a lesson in itself of no mean value.[2]

Manifestly, what we need is some means for studying the "causes of success or failure," some systematic way for analyzing, as Admiral Mahan urges, "the powers and limitations" of each new weapon.

Do we now have suitable organizations, methods, and procedures to do what Admiral Mahan asks us to do? The answer, however reluctantly given, appears to be no, we do not. To be sure, in the US Army Training and Doctrine Command (TRADOC), we have a major military organization explicitly dedicated to the preparation of doctrine. And TRADOC is abetted by a host of alphabetic agencies such as CATRADA (the Combined Arms Training Developments Activity), SCORES (Scenario-Oriented Recurring Evaluation System), and CDEC (Combat Developments Experimentation Command)—all of which have done interesting and valuable work. And, in addition, the faculties of the various Army schools are engaged in shaping doctrine.

These schools and agencies are staffed by hard-working and dedicated officers, many of them my friends, so what follows is not intended as a criticism of the individuals involved, only as an observation on the current state of doctrinal affairs.

There are many *organizations* addressing doctrinal problems, but how many of them have perfected adequate *procedures* to ensure that the doctrines produced represent only the most refined distillates from experience? Has any one of the organizations involved yet produced a document, a manual, a regulation, or a standing operating procedure that describes in comprehensive fashion the actual processes by which tactical doctrine is developed and assessed? One can find statements indicating which organizations are *responsible* but very little guidance on *how* the flow of *information* is *secured* and how the *analysis* is to be *conducted.*[3]

The task before us is clear. This article is a tentative effort to outline a procedure to chart the main steps in the development of doctrine. It can be no more than the opening statement in what should be a continuous dialogue as others comment, criticize, and contribute from different vantage points.

The first step is to pin down the key word, *doctrine.* Even a casual perusal of the literature will reveal that this term is often loosely employed, sometimes as if it were synonymous with "principle" and, at others, as if it were interchangeable with "concept." Doctrine is what is officially taught. It is an authoritative rule, a precept, giving the approved way to do a job. Doctrine represents the "tried and true"—the one best way to do the job—hammered out by trial and error, officially recognized as such, and then taught as the best way to achieve optimum results.

Marshal Ferdinand Foch, in *The Principles of War,* put it succinctly: "A complete military culture" is one in which military men have "examined and solved a number of concrete cases" on the basis of which they have derived a "doctrine or mental discipline which consists first in a common way of objectively approaching the subject; second, in a common way of handling it."[4]

Doctrine is derived by means of the intellectual process of generalization. This means one studies the evidence in a variety of cases, which is to say, experience that has been recorded. These instances are subjected to analysis, and, where neces-

7

sary, further experiments or trials may be carried out. By such means, which closely resemble the method of scientists, it should be possible to isolate and identify those practices that have, more or less consistently, produced the best results. The soundness of a generalization derived by such means is attested solely by the weight of the evidence, not by the rank or position of the individual who puts his authenticating imprimatur on the finished product.

The search for doctrine becomes a matter of discovering the best way to arrive at sound generalizations about tactics and technique. From extended study, it appears that there are three essential elements in this doctrinal process. These may be described as the *collection* phase, the *formulation* phase, and the *dissemination* phase, each of which merits close scrutiny.

The collection or information-gathering phase involves tapping the widest possible range of sources of information, some of which are enumerated below. First and foremost comes actual *combat experience* of our own armed forces as *recorded* by participants and observers. Note that I emphasize the word *recorded*. The term *experience* is elusive. Merely living through a combat operation is no guarantee that a participant derived any significant insights. One can almost say that experience is institutionally useful only when it is recorded. All of us probably agree that only battle can fully test a weapon or some novel scheme of tactics. Sometimes, however, a well-recorded exercise without bullets or blood has proved more useful in generating doctrine than a poorly recorded battle.

The recorded experience of *armies other than our own* is another obvious source, but there are many obstacles. The matrix of information so necessary to proper interpretation is never as full for foreign armies as it is for our own, and it is manifest that false inferences are more readily drawn from incomplete information. Moreover, the need for translations when working with most foreign armies injects yet another barrier. That serious—and successful—developers of military doctrine surmount this barrier is suggested by the report of how Gen Heinz Wilhelm Guderian paid out of his own pocket for a German translation of the official report on the 1934 British tank maneuvers because he was unwilling to wait for the Wehrmacht translation.[5]

Full-scale maneuvers are another important source of doctrinal information. By maneuver, we comprehend two-sided, free-play practice with a panoply of all arms. Such maneuvers are exceedingly costly and, therefore, infrequent. Their doctrinal payoff is directly proportional to the degree to which steps have been taken to test novel weapons or tactics. The lack of a fully effective relationship between those staging maneuvers and those responsible for the development of doctrine may be one of the weaker links in the armed forces today.

There are, of course, many obstacles to the successful exploitation of maneuvers. For one, anxiety over pleasing the high command is sometimes greater than zeal for the unvarnished truth. One is reminded of the occasion when King George V was observing a fleet maneuver and a radio-controlled, 80-mile-per-hour drone was flown in on an attack course to test the effectiveness of antiaircraft fire. Acutely embarrassed by the abysmally bad shooting of the defenders, the controller finally crashed the drone into the sea deliberately rather than let the king think it could fly through the fleet unscathed.[6]

Defects in the record resulting from inept or unwilling analysis on the part of participants also impair the value of maneuvers. In this connection, I recall the comment of one of my former students, an officer with extensive combat experience, who had occasion to study a large number of German army after-action reports just after he had done the same thing for his own service. His comments on the contrast between the two and the truly professional character of the German reports give one reason for concern.

The importance of maneuvers, it is well to remember, lies less in who "won" or scored the most points at the hands of the referees than with the insights derived and recorded by informed and thoughtful participants.[7] The dangers of misreading the results of maneuvers are ever-present. Gen George S. Patton, for example, was once criticized by the umpire for failing to mass his tanks according to the book; Patton was busy writing new doctrine that would avoid frontal assaults in favor of sweeping end runs to get astride the enemy line of communication.[8]

9

Valuable as maneuvers may be in developing new doctrine, at least one caveat is in order. It sometimes happens that a new weapon or a novel tactic being tried out in the course of a maneuver fails miserably precisely because it *is* new. Technological devices just emerging from the development cycle are seldom free of mechanical defects, and tactics that have not become routine have a distressing tendency to go awry.

In consequence, participants, unaware of the rudimentary character of the technology or tactics, may acquire an unwarranted prejudice against what is, in fact, a highly promising innovation, thereby dooming it despite its potential. In practice, it takes a good deal of imagination to see the real promise lurking in a decidedly imperfect trial version.

Unit exercises and service tests also may provide doctrinal information. However, such trials, in the absence of a full context of all arms, are unavoidably flawed as sufficient sources of doctrine. Even granting this limitation, however, much can be learned from exercises, *providing* the unit commander is allowed a free hand.

The point I am trying to make is that a true exercise or service test should not be confused with a mere demonstration. A *demonstration* is a set-piece operation, entirely preplanned. It allows little or no room for command initiative. Demonstrations can have a certain utility, but to put on a demonstration and call it an exercise is intellectual dishonesty.[9] The truly great senior commander in peacetime is the one who gives his subordinates "freedom to fail," rewarding imaginative initiative, even if it miscarries on occasion, while penalizing the "play it safe" subordinate who may "win" in the exercise but has ventured nothing and learns nothing.

War games, command post exercises, and the like—heads but no bodies—offer still another potential source of insights for the development of doctrine. Here, too, it may be said that games are useful to the extent they permit free play and initiative. The great shortcoming in much war gaming is the frequent absence of meticulous record keeping for close subsequent analysis, replay, and critique.[10] Such analysis is probably more important than the game play itself.

All of the foregoing—actual combat, maneuvers, exercises, and war games—are what historians would call the primary source materials for developing doctrine. But there are other sources of evidence of use in deriving sound generalizations on tactics and technique. This leads us to the necessity for providing the doctrinal organization with *a method for conducting* a continuous, comprehensive, and systematic *bibliographic search* of the available professional, historical, and technical literature.

For acceptable results, the doctrinal organization must have, or have access to, a competent staff using professionally prescribed procedures to garner information from published and unpublished sources, journals, monographs, memoirs, biographies, manuscript sources, and whatever else will shed light on the problem in hand. The institutional implications of this requirement are substantial: What is the optimum locale for such an agency? What are the necessary qualifications of the staff? What travel funds are essential for such a staff? What are their library and archival requirements?

Another dimension of the problem confronting a doctrinal staff is the need to provide continuous and *effective liaison* with appropriate agencies both inside and outside of the armed forces. What is the optimum form of liaison with the branch schools where doctrine is taught and often extensively developed? What is the most effective form of liaison with the operational research agencies and organizations, military and civilian? What form of liaison should be developed with the historical organizations of the services? And what ties should be developed with those universities where military history is studied seriously?

Information gathering or the *collection phase* is only the first of three separate steps. More difficult to describe in any brief account is the second or *formulation phase* during which doctrinal statements are actually devised, revised, and perfected.

The first point that needs to be made is elusive but crucially important. Before one sets about formulating doctrine, it is imperative that one's *frame of reference* (one's state of mind) is understood. It is dangerously easy to be unaware of *one's unstated assumptions.*

Does one set out to devise doctrine in a true spirit of unfettered scientific inquiry, or is one, perhaps unwittingly and un-

11

consciously, bowing to the preferences of a superior or simply the status quo. Here, it is appropriate to recall Norman Dixon's tale of the gunnery lieutenant in the Royal Navy who devised a highly promising modification in the control circuit. His captain declined to forward the proposal to higher headquarters. On asking why, he was informed, "the Admiral was the one who approved the existing arrangements and this would look like criticism of his decision."[11]

Readers will observe that my derogatory examples are usually drawn from foreign sources, all safely remote where one need not fear stepping too firmly on hypersensitive toes. It is well to learn this lesson early in life. A sign observed recently in a Pentagon office puts the problem bluntly: "A man who speaks the truth should keep one foot in the stirrup." In sum, one of the gravest dangers to be encountered in devising doctrine is the difficulty one may have in avoiding hierarchical pressures, *real or imagined,* when attempting to be truly objective. In a profession where complying with the will of one's superior is a way of life, true objectivity can be subtly elusive. Writing about this problem won't solve it, but forewarned may, in some degree, be forearmed.

Assuming that one is determined to be objective and has amassed an impressive array of recorded experience, how does he undertake the analysis that leads to sound generalization? The process is complex, but, in broad-brush terms, there are two essential steps. First, one undertakes a *systematic comparison of like experiences* to identify the common patterns of success. Then, secondly, one *deliberately searches for the unlike* or, as scientists would put it, the anomalous, the dissimilar experience which raises its own implicit challenge: Why?

The critical step in the formulation of doctrine is to devise procedures that consciously foster the dialectic, going out of one's way to seek contradictions, uncomfortable evidence which seems to confute the generalization, which may appear to flow most readily from the evidence.[12] This is probably one of the least developed features in the doctrinal process as it is now practiced by the armed forces.

Following analysis, one attempts to draft a tentative doctrinal statement. The mere act of writing induces a certain precision. It immediately reveals unresolved problems of terminology and definition. And, at some point, when the draft is in hand, one must candidly ask: Does this statement reflect the weight of the evidence? Is this, in fact, a sound generalization?

Now we are ready to verify our doctrinal statement with a trial balloon. Just as the theatrical producers in New York used to "try it in New Haven" before risking a run on Broadway, the formulators of military doctrine should spell out a doctrinal statement in a journal article, unofficially and informally, to elicit whatever response it may provoke. There are many advantages to a trial run. Being unofficial, it is unattributable; if it bombs, no one loses face. Moreover, publication in an open forum may elicit responses from wholly unexpected quarters. Professional journals should be the major vehicles for doctrinal discussion although experience has shown that editorial practices differ widely, and, in some journals, the dialogue is far more productive than in others. A professional journal that does not provoke and publish a lively response from its readers probably is only marginally effective. The requirement imposed on serving officers that they secure written approval from their superiors before publishing may not be regarded as censorship by those in command, but it would be difficult to deny that this stipulation has tended to inhibit full free discussion of at least some controversial military ideas.

Another form of trial balloon is to circulate the proposed draft within the *informal network*. By informal network, I mean the invisible college consisting of those individuals who are known to one another by correspondence and conversations. The collegiality arises from their association in a common enterprise, in this instance an interest in military doctrine. Members of the informal network exchange useful citations, reprints, rough drafts of their work in progress, stimulating thought, securing critical feedback, and the like. The enormous potential of the informal network has been demonstrated repeatedly in the scientific world. It merits wider emulation in military circles.

Yet another form of trial balloon is the *symposium*. A military symposium staged along the lines commonly stipulated in the academic world offers substantial potential for feedback on doctrinal propositions. There is a great impetus to productive

13

thought in paper deadlines. While it is often true that symposiums are better at provoking creativity and in fostering the free exchange of ideas than they are in producing close textual criticism, it is possible to structure a symposium so as to get the best of both. Where the former is advanced by periods of open, catch-as-catch-can audience participation, the latter is best achieved by formal panel critiques in which the panel members have been carefully chosen to ensure an in-depth analysis by competent specialists. The planning of a symposium panel is a professional undertaking of the most demanding sort. It also is one of the most necessary, for military organizations commonly lack built-in mechanisms for ensuring a rigorous critique of their work.

All the criticisms, new data, and other comments are fed back into the system for analysis leading to a *reformulation of the doctrinal statement.* It will be observed that the cast of our net in search of feedback has involved far more than the usual solicitation of replies by endorsement from a designated series of staff agencies. Such replies are essential, of course, but in themselves inadequate. However, when a doctrinal statement has been revised in the light of all the criticisms offered, simple prudence dictates the request for a second round of endorsements from all organizations directly concerned with the doctrinal matter.

This brings us to the *dissemination phase.* Here, the matter of format deserves more attention than it has received in doctrinal publications. Is it enough to make a doctrinal generalization baldly, with *no supporting factual evidence?* It may be useful on this point to recall William James's shrewd insight: "No one sees farther into a generalization than his own knowledge of the details extends."[13] Professor Thomas S. Kuhn, in *The Structure of Scientific Revolutions,* puts the same idea in a somewhat different way when he says, "the process of learning a theory depends upon the study of applications,"[14] all of which suggests that our doctrinal manuals may be fundamentally deficient. They normally offer unadorned generalizations, pure doctrine, without supporting evidence, historical examples, and the like to illustrate the experience on which the generalizations are based. While the supporting evidence or applications could be no more than illustrative, the requirement to include such matter would at the very least serve as a check on the more extreme forms of command influence on the formulation of doctrine without reference to the weight of the evidence.[15]

Anyone who is aware of the difference between the *United States Code* and the *United States Code Annotated** will appreciate the point I am trying to make. If it proves administratively unfeasible to publish all doctrinal manuals with illustrative examples and applications, perhaps some kind of annotated supplements could be devised. At the very least, doctrinal manuals should be documented so that the interested instructor in the service school and other similar users can replicate the reasoning and make use of the factual base of evidence from which the doctrinal writers derived their generalizations.

The armed forces doubtlessly would profess to be more scientific than theological. Yet as a matter of practice when offering unsupported and undocumented generalizations on matters of doctrine to their "followers," they are inviting belief as an act of faith rather than justifiable inferences on the basis of objective evidence open to independent scrutiny. Those who promulgate doctrine, disseminating it to the troops with its authoritative imprimatur, should not delude themselves that official sanction, fiat, by some automatic and inexorable process successfully internalizes the required message within the minds of all those who should be familiar with it. There are, after all, several kinds of doctrine. First, there is the official doctrine, complete with authenticating imprimatur, published in a manual. But then there is the unofficial kind, all those bits and pieces of doctrine in actuality—the doctrine, sound or erroneous, in the minds of men.

Let me illustrate the latter form of doctrine by quoting a passage from a study of doctrine written by a perceptive Army officer:

> One cannot base an analysis of doctrine solely on what is taught. To some, military doctrine signifies instructions such as those found in

---

*Editor's note: *US Code* is the official text of US statutes. *US Code Annotated* is a commercial publication that "combines official text of statutes with relevant case, historical notes, indexes, cross-references, and other annotations. It also includes the U.S. Constitution (annotated), selected *Code of Federal Regulations* provisions, presidential documents and federal court rules." [http://west.thomson.com/store/product. asp?product%5Fid=USCA]

> military manuals; but written doctrine is not always an accurate reflection of doctrine in practice. Expediency and tradition often compete with the written word as the loci of doctrine. The written word tends to reflect past experience, which may or may not be applicable to current circumstances. Extended expediency is capable of producing adjustments in doctrine that transcend the written word. And tradition is the keeper of that portion of doctrine that is so obvious to practitioners that it escapes confinement in print. The written word can be taught, but the contributions that come from expediency and tradition often fail to find their way into formal instruction.[16]

In strict parlance, the term *doctrine,* unless qualified by some modifier such as "unofficial" or "informal," should be restricted to fully approved and authenticated official doctrine.

Now and again, even official service manuals slip. Consider this splendid bit of heresy, for example, "doctrine is what the majority of the Army believes is right and is prepared to act on."[17] Surely, the guardians of the covenant were nodding when that one came up; its majoritarian implications run at least as far back as Plato's *Republic* where Thrasymachus defines justice as the interest of the stronger. On the other hand, had the statement been modified to read "in actual practice, effective doctrine is what the Army believes is right and is prepared to act on," the statement would have been a useful reminder that paper promulgations are not at all the same thing as lessons fully mastered by the troops.

Still another definition is one given me by an acute but light-hearted member of the US Army Command and General Staff College faculty some years ago. It says; "doctrine is lies all our fathers taught us." That is worth remembering because it serves to remind us that there is always a danger that doctrine will harden into dogma.

Among the everyday working definitions, the best I know of is one Gen John H. Cushman used some years ago when speaking to a group at Fort Leavenworth, Kansas: "Doctrine is an enlightened exposition of what has usually worked best."[18] I would modify that only by inserting "officially sanctioned" before the word "exposition." The phrase "what has usually worked best" captures almost perfectly the whole idea of doctrine as something based on objective assessment of recorded experience. It avoids dogmatism, yet it carries the implied authority of successful practice.

To recapitulate, I wish to stress the following point: We need to define and employ the term *doctrine* with greater precision. There are three phases in the development of military doctrine. In the *collection phase* we need to improve the cast of our net as we assemble objective information on tactics and technique. In the *formulation phase* we need to give greater thought to the intellectual process by which doctrinal generalizations are derived. At the same time we need to perfect the various devices, the trial balloons, which provide feedback on our tentative draft statements of doctrine. In the promulgation or *dissemination phase* we need to give more attention to the form and format in which doctrinal statements appear if we expect to persuade the rank and file that the doctrine proffered is sound and worth internalizing.

The foregoing admonishments are not addressed solely to those specialists assigned to the task of writing doctrine, but to military men in every echelon. Tactics and technique evolve out of the experience of all. It follows that all should understand the doctrinal process. And, in the spirit of John Dewey, we would be wise to recall that "real understanding comes not from passive observation but from intensive participation in the creative process."[19]

To conclude, let me revert to my opening quotation. It would appear that the lag that has characterized the development of military doctrine stems not from the "ignorance and formalism" of blimpish generals resisting innovation, but, rather, from a widespread failure to understand and to perfect the complex process of generalization by which sound doctrine is formulated. What has been suggested here is only an outline. This initial step will be of but limited effectiveness unless it provokes fruitful debate and elicits others' insights on the doctrinal process.

Notes

1. *Encyclopedia Britannica*, 1946 ed., s. v. "tactics."

2. Adm A. T. Mahan, *The Influence of Sea Power Upon History, 1660–1783* (Boston: Little, Brown & Co., 1918), 9–10.

3. Army Regulation (AR) 310-3, *Preparation, Coordination and Approval of Department of the Army Publications,* December 1968, with changes. Chapter 7 spells out responsibilities for training literature along with TRADOC Supplement 1 to AR 310-3, 10 February 1975; TRADOC Regulation 71-4 on standard scenarios, 19 October 1973; TRADOC Regulation 71-5, *Scenario Oriented Recurring Evaluation System (SCORES),* 14 February 1975; and AR 5-5, *The Army Study System,* 26 June 1974, all devote more attention to defining responsibility than to blueprinting the analytical procedures to be employed.

4. Gen Ferdinand Foch, *The Principles of War* (London: Chapman & Halt, 1918), 18.

5. B. H. Liddell Hart, *The Liddell Hart Memoirs,* vol. 1 (New York: G. P., Putnam's Sons, 1965), 247.

6. Ibid., 331.

7. Harold R. Winton, *To Change an Army: General Sir John Burnett-Stuart and British Armor Doctrine, 1927–1938* (Lawrence, Kans.: University Press of Kansas, 1988), 182.

8. Martin Blumenson, *Patton Papers: 1940–1945,* vol. 2 (Boston: Houghton-Mifflin, 1974), 37.

9. Lt Gen William Balck, *Development of Tactics* (Fort Leavenworth, Kans.: General Service School Press, 1922), 2–3.

10. Adm Harris Laning, "The Naval War College Year," *Naval War College Review* (March 1969), 74–78.

11. K. G. B. Dewar, *The Navy from Within,* cited in Norman Dixon, *On the Psychology of Military Incompetence* (New York: Basic Books, 1976), 270.

12. Dialectic is a method of inquiry, a discussion in which the goal of the participants is to achieve understanding. Contrast this with eristic discussion (from Eris, the goddess of strife), which involves argument, each participant striving to win.

13. William James, *Letters* (Boston: Little, Brown & Co., 1926), 65.

14. Thomas S. Kuhn, *The Structure of the Scientific Revolution* (Chicago: University of Chicago Press, 1970), 46–47.

15. The notion that soldiers who are shown the evidence behind a given military policy will be readier to contribute constructively from their experiences is illustrated by Sir John Monash who confronted one of the major doctrinal crises of the World War I era. I am indebted to Professor Theodore Ropp for this citation as well as for trenchant criticism of an earlier draft of this article. See A. J. Smithers, *Sir John Monash* (London: Leo Cooper, 1973), 211–19.

16. Maj Vardell E. Nesmith, "Stagnation and Change in Military Thought: The Evolution of Field Artillery Doctrine of the United States Army, 1861–1905" (unpublished paper, Duke University, Durham, N.C., 1977), 59.

17. TRADOC Bulletin No. 5, *Weapons, Tactics, Training: Training with LAW* (Fort Monroe, Va.: US Army Training and Doctrine Command, June 1976), 5.

18. Combined Arms Center and Fort Leavenworth Pamphlet no. 1, Maj Gen John H. Cushman, "The CGSC Approach to Writing to Doctrinal Literature" (Fort Leavenworth, Kans., 1973), 3.

19. J. DeH. Mathews, "Arts and the People . . .," *Journal of American History,* September 1975, 322–23.

Essay 3

Concepts, Doctrines, Principles*

Baron Antoine-Henri Jomini in his famous study on the art of war, which attempted to identify the essentials of Napoleon's military genius, devoted many pages to the task of defining key terms such as *strategy, tactics,* and the like.[1] He grasped the fundamental notion that without uniform definitions, clearly understood, the search for sound military practice is certain to be seriously flawed.

Unfortunately, Jomini's good advice all too frequently has been ignored in recent years by military writers. One encounters articles equating doctrine with "the philosophy of war" while still others refer to doctrine as "concepts and principles" as if all three terms were interchangeable. This confusion even extends to such official promulgations as Joint Chiefs of Staff Publication (JCS Pub) 1, *Dictionary of US Military Terms for Joint Usage,* which has at one time or another identified doctrine as "a combination of principles and policies" (1949 edition) or as "fundamental principles" (1979 edition). Such definitions are at the very least confusing when not downright erroneous. There is, then, much to be gained from a concerted effort to achieve precision and uniformity when employing key military terminology.

What is a concept? To conceive an idea is to formulate it in words in the mind. In the mind it is notional; it exists only as a theory, an idea yet unproved. To conceptualize is to devise a mental construct, a picture in the brain that eventually is expressed in words. It is speculative, tentative. To illustrate the notion of a concept, let us go back to World War I. In the early days of that war, pilots from opposing sides at first largely ignored one another on chance encounters in the air. Eventually they armed their airplanes with machine-guns, but they soon

---

*This chapter originally appeared as an article in the *Air University Review* 35 (July 1984). It reflects the author's reaction to the frequent misuse of the terms encountered in official and unofficial publications, especially the tendency to employ "doctrine" and "principles" as if they were entirely interchangeable and synonymous.

discovered that it was exceedingly difficult to hit a high-speed target from a moving platform. We can readily visualize one of the more creative individuals among them reflecting on the problem: If I were to attack from dead astern, the enemy pilot would be far less liable to see me approach and there would be no deflection, no relative motion of the target in my sights, so it ought to be easier to make a kill with fewer shots. This mental image or concept in the reflective pilot's mind is a hypothesis, a conjectural conception to be proved true or false by trial and error.

In contrast to a concept, what is doctrine? Doctrines are what is taught. Doctrine consists of rules or procedures drawn by competent authority. Doctrines are precepts, guides to action, suggested methods for solving problems or attaining desired results.

Clearly there is a marked difference between concepts and doctrines. Concepts spring from creative imagination. A perceptive observer draws an inference from one or more observed facts. A primitive man observes the springiness in a bent bough and infers that the thrust might be capable of projecting a missile; eventually this initial conception, this tentative idea, leads to the bow and arrow, a major advance in the weaponry of mankind. So too the World War I pilot who first thought of attacking from dead astern came up with an innovative idea, a working hypothesis. In each instance the concept or hypothesis had to be tried in practice to confirm or confute the inference drawn by the reflective observer.

Doctrine, on the other hand, is an officially approved teaching based upon accumulated experience, numerous recorded instances that have led to a generalization. To generalize is to infer inductively a common pattern from repeated experiences that have produced the same or similar results. In World War I, as more and more pilots tried attacking from above, astern, and out of the sun, they found the probability of making a kill tended to rise rapidly. On the basis of such experiences, reinforced by repetition, those who instructed neophyte pilots generalized this common pattern of attack into informal doctrine. Eventually, when blessed with official sanction, this informal doctrine became enshrined in manuals bearing the official imprimatur as formal doctrine.

Where a concept is a hypothesis—an inference that suggests that a proposed pattern of behavior *may possibly* lead to a desired result, a doctrine is a generalization based on sufficient evidence to suggest that a given pattern of behavior *will probably* lead to the desired result. Where a concept is tentative and speculative, a doctrine is more assured. Doctrines are akin to rules, precepts or maxims, a set of operations or moves reduced to more or less uniform procedures for meeting specific types of problems. Of course, in actual military practice no hard and fast rules or maxims can be followed slavishly and mechanically in every instance with complete assurance that the anticipated and desired result will ineluctably follow. Because there are so many variables and imponderables in any military situation, doctrines must never be regarded as absolutes. Perhaps the best definition holds doctrine as that mode of approach that repeated experience has shown usually works best.

Just as concepts are not to be confused with doctrines, so too must doctrines be distinguished from principles. Principles, as Aristotle pointed out long ago, are truths that are evident and general. One can lay down a rule, somewhat arbitrarily, based on observed experience: when attacking, come out of the sun. On the other hand, one cannot lay down a principle arbitrarily; one can only declare it. Rules, and hence doctrines, are within the power of properly constituted military authority; principles are not.

Where doctrines are derived by generalization, taking many cases and finding the common pattern, principles are derived by abstraction. Abstraction involves taking a single instance and distilling out its essence. The essence or epitome is that part which typically represents the whole. For this reason principles are commonly expressed as axioms. Axioms are universally received self-evident truths.

The principles of war, more accurately termed the principles of battle, rest upon close study of individual engagements. The process of abstraction has been carried to the point where single words or brief phrases such as "surprise," "concentration," "initiative," or "economy of force" epitomize the principles discerned in the mass of detail. With doctrine, the thrust is on "how to do it." With principle, on the other hand, the thrust is to explain the underlying idea.

What, one may ask, is the principle of battle involved in the doctrinal injunction to attack from high astern and out of the sun? From astern one's approach not only avoids a deflection shot but is less liable to be observed because of the limitations human anatomy imposes on the craning neck of a pilot scanning the sky for potential enemies. From out of the sun further reduces the probability of being detected. By approaching from high above, the attacker acquires added acceleration from his dive, giving a margin of advantage, among other ways, by shortening the time of closing. However, all of these factors are but means to an end. The essential principle involved is surprise. The attacker seeks to catch his prey unawares. Modern electronic means may alter the doctrine and suggest new patterns of attack, but the principle will remain unchanged. More than one principle could be involved in any single situation, but for purposes of illustration we need only consider here the principle of surprise.

Concepts, doctrines, and principles are entirely different terms and are not to be used interchangeably. To simplify the task of mastering these words, the ideas explicated above are presented in synoptic fashion in figure 1.

Notes

1. Brig Gen J. D. Hittle, *Jomini and His Summary of the Art of War* (Harrisburg, Pa.: 1958), 10.

	CONCEPT	DOCTRINE	PRINCIPLE
DEFINITION:	Hypothesis; an innovative idea; a tentative conceptualization; a debatable proposal	Precept; an authoritative rule; a method officially taught; a maxim for action	Axiom; an epitome or essence
COLLOQUIAL DEFINITION:	Trial and error	Tried and true	Self-evident truth
DERIVATION:	By inference from individual observation	By generalization through study of recorded accumulated experience	By abstraction through heuristic analysis of individual instances
END SOUGHT:	To propose an innovation or to modify existing practice	To establish procedures for optimum performance	To inform for better understanding; never directive, only illuminating
AUTHORSHIP:	Any perceptive observer who formulates and publishes his or her conceptualization	Promulgated by designated staff officers at the behest of command	Military scholars
AUTHORITY:	Unofficial; on individual initiative, informal	Official; by weight of the evidence systematically studied; authenticated by fiat and imprimatur	Validated only by long use and widespread acceptance
STYLE:	Argumentative, persuasive	Prescriptive, didactic, affirmative	Declaratory, expositive
CHARACTERISTIC FORMAT:	Journal article or staff study	Regulation or manual	Word or phrase
MEASURE OF EFFECTIVENESS:	Extent to which it stimulates thought	Extent to which promulgated doctrine is applied with success in actual practice	Extent to which it facilitates and illuminates the decision-making process

Figure 1. Terminology Matrix

THIS PAGE INTENTIONALLY LEFT BLANK

Essay 4

Some Seminal Thinkers on Technology and Doctrine*

Because the fall of France in the spring of 1940 was such a soul-searing event for so many of our generation, it offers a fitting point of departure for a discussion of technology and doctrine as viewed by some seminal theorists. Contrary to the popular notion, the French Army in the between-war years did not abandon its belief that offensive action would be necessary. The Maginot line was a prudent investment to provide extensive security across France's exposed border to allow a concentration of offensive forces at the critical point.[1] By May of 1940, the French and British armies in France had more tanks than did the Germans, and many of them were excellent vehicles of the latest design.[2]

Unfortunately for the fate of France, her army leaders had promulgated a doctrine that called for a carefully orchestrated attack—step by step within rigidly controlled divisional boundaries—by phased advances in which air, armor, and artillery all functioned in a tightly controlled harmony. This was an updated version of the kind of war that had been perfected by the end of 1918. It was the exact opposite of the German concept of blitzkrieg, which stressed individual initiative, opportunistic exploitation of unexpected openings and local vulnerabilities in the French lines. The German army service manual on troop leadership in use immediately prior to World War II reflected an attitude quite different from the French view: "War undergoes continual evolution. New arms give ever-new forms to combat. To foresee this technical evolution before it occurs, to judge well the influence of these new arms on battle, to employ them before others is an essential condition for success."[3] In short, the

*This essay was originally presented at the 15th Annual Conference of the Security Studies Program, Tufts University, in 1986. It was subsequently published as chapter 2 in a volume titled *Emerging Doctrines and Technologies* (Lexington, Mass., D.C. Heath & Company, 1988), edited by Robert L. Pfaltzgraff Jr., Uri Ra'anan, Richard H. Schultz Jr., and Igor Lukes, whom the author thanks for permission to reprint in this anthology.

French lost because they had adopted a faulty doctrine. Manifestly, then, doctrine was of crucial importance.[4]

But what is doctrine? Military doctrine is an officially approved teaching, a precept, a guide to action, a suggested method for solving problems or attaining desired results. Military doctrines are based upon accumulated experience—numerous recorded examples that have led to the formulation of a generalization, which is to say an inductive inference from repeated experiences that have produced similar results. But doctrines are not hard-and-fast rules to be slavishly applied; they are suggestive. Perhaps the best definition of military doctrine is "that mode of approach which repeated experience has shown usually works best."[5]

The problems of formulating military doctrine are enormously complicated by advances in technology. What may have been sound doctrine yesterday (firmly grounded in repeated experiences carefully recorded and analyzed) can become obsolete almost overnight when technological innovations are unexpectedly introduced. There is an ever-present danger that doctrine will be allowed to harden into dogma when military men fail to appreciate the implications of a technological advance that holds great potential for reshaping the character of warfare. Here I explore the experience of several military theorists and thinkers who have recognized the significance of such crucial technological shifts and have attempted to reorient prevailing doctrinal notions. An account of their successes and failures may afford us some insights on ways to improve the doctrinal process to accommodate more successfully in our own day to technological novelties.

Anyone turning to the pages of Carl von Clausewitz will be startled to discover how little attention he devotes to the implications that technological advances in weaponry have had for armies. Even though Clausewitz wrote when the Industrial Revolution was already underway, he still asserted that arming and equipping are not essential to the conception of fighting and seldom affect strategy.[6] As Liddell Hart has observed, Clausewitz continued to see numbers, manpower, as decisive, even as his world was entering a great age of machine power.[7] For that matter, most of the classical military thinkers and theorists from Sun Tzu to Baron Henri-Antoine Jomini have in much the same way tended to take technology for granted.[8]

Probably the least recognized seminal thinker in the realm of military doctrine and technology was a contemporary of Clausewitz: Sir William Congreve—a highly imaginative officer who subsequently became a member of the Royal Society. As a colonel of artillery, while serving at the Royal Laboratory at Woolwich in 1805, he developed the famous rocket that bears his name, perfecting a device used against the British some twenty years earlier by the soldiers of a prince in India. Congreve's rocket was a relatively crude black-powder affair, a cylindrical canister mounted on a sixteen-foot stick. While not very accurate, it achieved ranges up to two miles, enough to warrant its use against the French at Boulogne in 1805, at Copenhagen in 1806, and in several battles on the continent, not to mention its success against the Americans at Bladensburg [Maryland] in 1814. Although "the rockets' red glare" at Fort McHenry has been immortalized in our national anthem, the novel weapon failed to ensure victory there. The Congreve rocket had, however, demonstrated sufficient utility to warrant royal approval for the formation of a rocket corps as an adjunct of the Royal Artillery.[9] It was at this juncture that Congreve demonstrated his capacity as a doctrinal thinker—as distinct from his role as an inventor or designer—when he published (in 1814) a little booklet entitled:

> The Details of the Rocket System shewing the Various Applications of this weapon both for sea and land service and its different uses in the field and in sieges. Illustrated by plates of the principal equipments, exercizes and cases of actual service. With general instructions for its application and a demonstration of the comparative economy of the system. Drawn up by Colonel William Congreve for the information of the officers of the rocket corps, and others whom it may concern.[10]

Congreve's elongated title, in typical eighteenth-century fashion, serves as an abstract for the whole volume. The most revealing word in the title is *system*, for Congreve had a thorough grasp of what we today call a weapon system—an idea that did not come fully into focus until after World War II. If the title leaves the reader breathless, it nonetheless reveals the full contents of the document: the research and development involved in the

27

design; detailed statements of tactical doctrine for the application of rocket volleys; minute particulars as to the training of rocket troops; a careful delineation of the necessary tables of organization and equipment down to the last little particular such as lance heads threaded in such a way as to be screwed on the sixteen-foot rocket poles and used in an emergency as lances by the mounted rocket troops. And finally, a careful cost-benefit analysis is offered in comparison with conventional artillery.[11]

By the middle of the eighteenth century, improvements in conventional artillery had left the rocket far behind, but for our purposes this is of no moment. Congreve's publication is important because it reflects his thorough understanding of the role of doctrine in assisting a technological innovation in finding its rightful place in a nation's array of weaponry. He offered his work, as he explained in his introduction, not only "for the instruction of the officers of the corps" but also "for the information of the General Officers of the British Army" as well as "such departments as need to know the good of the service," acquainting them with "the principles of this new branch," which had already been demonstrated in combat and had "given pledges of future and greater successes." Here was a man who understood the importance of using evidence of successful tactical performance to convince doubters, the importance of persuading those in command as well as those in the tactical units and the supply bureaus.

Here was an almost ideal model for emulation in the development of military doctrine to accommodate a technological innovation. Unfortunately, at least from the standpoint of the effectiveness of the British army, it seems to have had little impact. Congreve's work stands as the product of isolated genius, never institutionalized or incorporated into the routine procedures and practices of the British forces.[12]

In Germany there was a rather different pattern of response to the problems raised by advancing technology. Although there were several systematic military theorists in nineteenth-century Germany, Moltke the elder* probably affords us more insights than any other into the problem of accommodating

---

*Field Marshal Helmuth Karl Bernhard, Graf von Moltke

doctrine to technology. If for no other reason, his unusually long period of influence (he was chief of staff for king and emperor for 30 years from 1858 to 1888) provided him opportunities to implement and institutionalize his ideas in a way that Congreve (whose commission, incidentally, was in the Hanoverian army, not the British army) never could.[13]

Unlike Congreve, Moltke was the fortunate heir of the new professionalism of the Prussian army growing out of the reforms of Stein, Scharnhorst, and Gneisenau.* Soon after he joined the Prussian army in 1822, Moltke attended the Kriegs Akademie, already a thriving institution reflecting Scharnhorst's genius. But Moltke's military education involved far more than academic studies. He traveled widely, mastered six or seven languages, and served four years on leave from the Prussian army as military adviser to the pasha of Turkey, where he saw action in the field. A tour of duty as an aide to Prince Frederic William led to his appointment as chief of staff when his patron became King Frederick III of Prussia.[14]

At the time of his appointment as chief of staff, Moltke had never commanded any formation larger than a battalion, and that was in garrison. Nonetheless, he was well served by his broad education and fine qualities of mind. As early as 1843 he had written an essay on the factors to be considered in selecting routes to be followed in laying down the rapidly expanding German railway net, perceptively anticipating their military significance. Manifestly, Moltke had a high degree of open-mindedness and intellectual curiosity. But for our purposes, in seeking to understand the link between advancing technology and military doctrine, Moltke's professional military education provides the essential clues to understanding his significant contributions.

Thanks to the genius of Scharnhorst, the institution, which came to be called the Kriegs Akademie, had already begun to teach not only the necessity of formulating standard doctrine but also the need for a systematic process for deriving that doctrine from experience. As Scharnhorst visualized the process,

---

*Heinrich Friedrich Karl Reichsfreihern vom and zum Stein (Karl vom Stein), Gerhard Johann David vom Scharnhorst, August Count (Graf) Neidhardt vom Gneisenau

it consisted of a series of well-defined steps. First came the formation of a commission of able officers representing all arms of the service to ensure an adequate appreciation of the wider dimensions of the problem. This commission would then formulate a conceptual outline of the undertaking as a point of departure. Thus oriented, reports would be elicited from operational units in the field army. The ideas thus derived would then be subjected to tests and experiments by the commission in its inquiry. At the same time, the members of the commission would endeavor to saturate themselves in the better-known writings on the art of war and the history of the most instructive campaigns to understand the evolution of doctrine down to the present. Finally, Scharnhorst went a step further to ensure objectivity and impartiality; he proposed assigning the same doctrinal problem to two different sets of officers working independently.[15]

As historian Peter Paret has pointed out, Scharnhorst believed that every aspect of the military art, from a musket to an army, was subject to improvement by experiments revealing its *potential* in contrast to the accepted design or practice. Scharnhorst spelled this out in his widely used *Handbüch der Artillerie:* "Theory instigates suggestions for improvements, experiments assist in the first investigation, and additional experience or large-scale application serves to confirm their usefulness. In this way, improvements in artillery take place, which thus comes ever nearer to perfection."[16] In short, when Moltke entered the Prussian army he found there a well-developed conception of what doctrine is and remarkably well-defined procedures for deriving it.

The crushing defeat that the outnumbered Prussians inflicted on the Austrians at Königgrätz in 1866 significantly enhanced Moltke's stature as chief of staff. Historians have credited the Dreyse breech-loading needlegun as an important factor in that victory, as indeed it was. Although the needlegun had considerably less range than a muzzle-loading rifle firing minié bullets, it could fire seven shots for every two of the muzzle-loader. This was a decided advantage—giving greater firepower with fewer men—but it was another characteristic that gave the needlegun its greatest tactical advantage. As a breech-loader, it could be fired from a prone position, which is to say from a well-protected defensive site. The Austrian forces, committed to an offensive tactical doctrine that relied upon the bayonet charge to break the enemy, were cut down by all-but-invisible Prussians with their needleguns.[17] This was a stunning technological innovation accompanied by an appropriate adjustment in tactical doctrine. Although Moltke had nothing to do with the initial decision to adopt the needlegun, he quickly perceived its tactical implications and resolved to exploit them in the subsequent war with France. By pairing his strategic offensive with a tactical defense that would take advantage of the French faith in élan and the bayonet, Moltke was able to repeat the earlier Prussian success at Königgrätz.[18]

Far more than most of his contemporaries, Moltke sensed the profound significance of the railroad and the telegraph for the art of war. From his close study of the US Civil War he understood that improved transportation and communication made possible by these technological advances freed the army from reliance upon the seasonally impassable road network and made possible concentric operations by which widely scattered units could achieve surprise by concentrating at the critical point with great rapidity and thus take the enemy in detail.[19]

While Moltke was not the first to exploit the railroad and the telegraph for military purposes, it was he who developed the doctrine that made possible their successful application. Building on the foundations laid by Scharnhorst and his fellow reformers, Moltke endeavored to develop the General Staff into what Spenser Wilkinson aptly called the brain of the army. He clearly understood that the vast aggregations of forces made possible by the use of railroads—a quarter of a million men converging on the Austrians at Königgrätz—would be far too unwieldy for a single commander to control. Only with the aid of a well-trained staff could such numbers be exploited effectively.[20]

Just promulgating appropriate doctrine was not enough. Moltke understood that staffs have to be perfected by repeated trials. He conducted test mobilizations, which revealed imperfections in the plans and less than gratifying performance by inexperienced officers. Despite royal reprimands and other such pressures, some officers made the same mistakes in the practice maneuvers two years in a row. Moltke's genius lay in applying

31

Scharnhorst's emphasis on a careful recording of experience, which he then analyzed with utter objectivity to produce viable doctrine. This procedure he inculcated successfully in the able group of officers trained at the Kriegs Akadamie and subsequently selected for General Staff duty.[21]

While Moltke's appreciation of the potential in the new technology and his ability to develop appropriate doctrines to exploit it are decidedly impressive, it would be a mistake to assume that the campaign against Austria in 1866 moved along with clockwork efficiency. The doctrine, which is crystal clear in the mind of the commander or in the understanding of his gifted and professionally educated General Staff officers, inevitably seems to get leached out when it is to be applied by far less well-trained troops in the field. Furthermore, Clausewitz's fog of war—the accidents and misunderstandings— inescapably complicates reality.

Moltke had more than a quarter-million men in three armies spread over some 260 miles of front to ensure the widest possible range of strategic options to respond to the yet unknown deployment of the enemy. According to the well-conceived doctrine, the telegraph would allow the commander in Berlin to control the point and pace by which these three armies would converge. To be fully effective, however, doctrine cannot be limited to the general level of application alone. The troops, clear down to the point man at the head of the advancing columns, need detailed doctrinal guidance. That this tactical level of "telegraph doctrine" had not yet been perfected almost immediately became evident.

Although Moltke used the telegraph with good effect to regulate the flow of rail traffic while deploying the Prussian forces to the Austrian frontier, difficulties began to crop up as the troops pressed into enemy territory. During the 1850s the Prussians had experimented with wagon-mounted portable telegraphs and by 1865 had established well-equipped field telegraph service units. These were capable of stringing two or three miles of wire an hour and sending out eight or ten words a minute as they followed advancing troop units.[22] Unfortunately while the telegraphers were well trained, the men in the combat arm were not adequately aware of the ramifications of the novel instruments. As they advanced deeper into Austria, they not only destroyed the enemy telegraph lines but also happily added the dry poles to their campfires. As a consequence, when Prussian telegraph wagons arrived on the scene they had great difficulty in stringing their lines. Problems of this sort injected hours and sometimes days of delay before tactical commanders at the front were in direct communication with the theater commander. On an average, some 12 hours elapsed between the issuing of a telegraphic order and its execution.[23]

Much the same thing happened with the railroads out at the tactical level. Although a railroad section had been established in the Prussian General Staff as early as 1864, the doctrine developed by this unit dealt with the strategic deployment of forces.[24] In mobilizing for the Danish war, the railroads deployed troops in six days where road marching would have required 16. The savings in rations and payroll thus achieved more than offset the cost of the transportation.[25] At the tactical level, however, just as with the telegraph, the absence of well-developed doctrine led to numerous breakdowns, especially in the supply system.

Whereas the General Staff officers had planned minutely and effectively for the strategic deployment of troops, they had failed to provide guidance to those out at the end of the line. As supply trains were regularly dispatched from the depots, it turned out that inadequate provision had been made to unload the freight cars at the railhead. Sidings soon jammed with idled cars; the materiel they carried was not off-loaded in a timely manner, in part because quartermaster officers, lacking adequate field storage for perishable foodstuffs, used freight cars as substitute warehouses, thus compounding the problem by failing to return empties for use elsewhere.[26]

Perhaps the most impressive feature of the German staff system was its ability to learn from its mistakes. As soon as the Austrians had been crushed, Moltke set to work seeking to remedy the doctrinal flaws revealed by experience. In this effort he was well served by the staff system that had evolved out of the reforms of Scharnhorst and his successors. Only the ablest graduates of the Kriegs Akademie were assigned to the General Staff.

After duty there, they were sent down for duty with troops to ensure that they remained in touch with the harsh realities of the operational units. Those who did well with troops would be promoted much sooner than their contemporaries and recalled to duty with the Great General Staff. This system not only provided powerful incentives to sustained excellence, but established a mechanism by which there was continual selection of the ablest officers. Furthermore, the rotation of highly qualified officers trained to think objectively meant that the chief of staff had a network of reliable observers out at the operational level who routinely reported where and how the system was malfunctioning and what doctrinal improvement was needed.[27]

In short, Moltke made effective use of the well-contrived Prussian staff system to devise appropriate doctrines to exploit the technological advances available to him. The doctrinal product in this particular situation was a route service regulation issued in 1867 but kept secret until it was employed against the French in 1870. While this represented a substantial advance over the guidance offered in the deployment of 1866 against the Austrians, once more when put into practice even this improved doctrine revealed numerous shortcomings, and the cycle began all over again as Moltke set his staff to analyzing the mistakes that had been made.[28]

If we turn now to another seminal thinker, one who did not have the advantage afforded by the well-articulated staff system of the Prussians, it should be possible to make some useful comparisons. Before the outbreak of war in 1914, Col J. F. C. Fuller of the British army had already shown himself to be an unusually thoughtful officer. From an extensive but close reading of Napoleon's correspondence, he had deduced what he believed were the enduring principles of war. Clearly, here was a military intellectual. In 1916 Fuller was transferred to the Tank Corps, then known as the heavy machine-gun corps since tanks were conceived as armored machine-gun carriers. There he became enamored of the largely untapped potential of these remarkable new engine-powered land cruisers. But where most other tank enthusiasts thought in terms of the tangible, Fuller's disciplined mind promptly considered the future of armor abstractly. As Basil H. Liddell Hart subsequently assessed him, Fuller was neither a good administrator nor a good commander but "just what a good staff officer ought to be, evolving sound ideas and leaving the execution to others."[29]

By way of illustration, Fuller supplied his general, Sir Henry Wilson, with the facts and figures to present a strong case to the War Department for building a tank army. He based his case on careful operational research. At Messines, where 12 divisions attacked on a 16,500-yard front, they penetrated 4,500 yards in 48 hours and lost 16,000 men. Contrasting this performance was the assault at Cambrai using tanks; there, seven divisions on a 13,500-yard front penetrated 9,000 yards in 48 hours with a loss of 9,500 men.[30]

There was, however, more to Fuller's genius than an ability to assemble facts in defense of tanks as a revolutionary new weapon. He perceived that the speed and mobility of the tank opened up an entirely new strategic vista. While observing the near collapse of the British forces under the German assaults of March 1918, he realized that an army headquarters in hurried retreat loses contact with its troops, and this leads to chaos. From this observation he reasoned that the road to victory was to devise tactics to accomplish just this. Enemy fighting strength lies in its cohesive organization. To destroy this cohesion is to destroy its fighting ability. This destruction can be accomplished by attrition, slowly grinding down the whole organization. But Fuller saw that there was an important alternative: design an attack that would "unhinge" the enemy. The former approach he compared to killing a man by inflicting many slight wounds until he bleeds to death; the latter was akin to a single fatal shot to the brain. Armored forces, said Fuller, should penetrate rapidly through the lines of a salient and seek out and destroy the enemy headquarters, which would literally unhinge the now leaderless units at the front. This conception was the underlying doctrine reflected in his "Plan 1919," which, in July 1918, called for an armored striking force of some 12,500 tanks.[31]

Since there was scant possibility of producing more than 12,000 tanks in time for the proposed scheme (even if it secured the approval of the cavalry generals such as Douglas Haig), little came of this scheme. Fuller, who was transferred from France to the War Office in August 1918, continued his drive to win greater recognition for the tank. He did this largely by means of an informal publication, *Weekly Tank Notes,* which he used as a platform to push his innovative doctrinal views—as he expressed it—"to educate the generals."[32]

Up to this point Fuller seems to have made all the right moves. He built his case with factual evidence, he devised a vehicle to see that his ideas reached the proper authorities, the men of influence (he was pleased when the king himself asked to be put on the distribution list for *Weekly Tank Notes*). When he wrote, he displayed a genuine gift for the well-turned phrase and the persuasive illustration.

For example, in making the case that weapons were the key to victory, he illustrated his contention with a telling assertion. Napoleon, he said, was an inherently abler general than Lord Raglan.* Yet Lord Raglan's army in 1855 would surely have beaten any army Napoleon could have led because Raglan's men were armed with the minié rifle. But then, in what was to become a nearly fatal tendency to overstatement, Fuller went on to say: "Tools or weapons, if only the right ones can be discovered, form 99% of victory. Strategy, command, leadership, courage, discipline, supply, organization and all the moral and physical paraphernalia of war are nothing to a high superiority of weapons—at most they go to form the one percent which makes the whole possible."[33]

Although the British did establish a Royal Tank Corps on a permanent basis, Fuller's imaginative and innovative proposals for a revolutionary doctrine for armored warfare were largely ignored. Once the war ended, the inexorable pressure to cope with an aggressive enemy relaxed. Severe reductions in funding made meaningful development of tanks difficult if not impossible. Worse yet, constraints on funding brought out the worst in branch rivalries as each sought to defend its all-too-meager share of the annual appropriation. It was in this context that Fuller wrote his now famous prize essay in the *Journal* of the Royal United Services Institute.[34]

---

*FitzRoy James Henry Somerset

Fuller's gold-medal essay was entitled "The Application of Recent Developments in Mechanics and other Scientific Knowledge to Preparation and Training for Future War on Land."[35] In an apparent effort to sustain the impetus achieved by tanks in the war and at the same time appeal to his horse-loving contemporaries, he headed his essay with the motto: "Racehorses don't pull up at the winning post." What followed was a carefully reasoned exposition of his doctrinal ideas for effective exploitation of the latent capabilities of the tank.

Unfortunately, the colonel could not control his propensity for the caustic remark. He excoriated the "old school" soldier who, "in the words of Erasmus, is only too prone to identify the new learning with heresy and so make orthodoxy synonymous with ignorance."[36] He compounded his jibes by going on to suggest that a properly developed tank army would "replace entirely the horsemen" and also the infantry.[37]

The wave of vituperative reaction that such remarks brought down on Fuller from the disgruntled fox-hunting cavalrymen resulted in an almost total neglect of his carefully formulated specifications for an elaborate staff system for producing doctrinal manuals—no such coherent procedure then existed in the British army. What Fuller described was much akin to what the Germans had already accomplished. He wanted not only doctrinal manuals for senior commanders and manuals for troop leaders, but also manuals for "the led." Perhaps most important of all, he called for staff manuals that would give doctrinal guidance to "show how Staff work cements the whole together."[38]

Although Fuller eventually became a major general, he never received any significant command, which is hardly surprising for one who referred to Haig as "a stone-age general" and the War Office as "a glutinous mass."[39] He retired in 1933 at the relatively young age of 54. Thereafter, though he continued to publish voluminously, he was an outsider and his views had little discernable influence on official doctrine. Ironically, if his British contemporaries largely ignored him, he was heeded abroad, especially in Germany, where his ideas were absorbed, even if often indirectly through the writings of his most important disciple, Liddell Hart. Though less given to caustic personal criticism, Liddell Hart for all his gifts remained for most of his career an outsider, resented by those military men who feared his brand of critical journalism.[40]

In two respects Fuller—and Liddell Hart—failed. Despite Fuller's perceptive call for the creation of a carefully structured system for deriving doctrine, there is little or no evidence that it led to any institutional adoption of such a system in the British Army. And, when that army finally was forced to rearm in reaction to the rising menace of fascist dictatorships on the continent, the ratio of tank divisions to infantry divisions was one to seven. Which is to say, the British Army was planning to fight a manpower war rather than the mechanized war soon to be unleashed as blitzkrieg by Hitler. Of the two failures, it may be argued that the latter was the more serious. Wehrmacht successes would win many converts to armored warfare, but in failing to heed Fuller's call for a fully articulated process for perfecting doctrine, the British deprived themselves of a vital tool for keeping abreast of advancing technology in weaponry.[41]

In many ways the career of Gen Giulio Douhet—the exponent of airpower—ran parallel to that of General Fuller. Born in 1869, the year Jomini died, Douhet entered the Italian military academy, where he graduated first in his class. Subsequent study at the Polytechnic Institute in Turin rounded off his formal education. After service on the General Staff he took command of an elite Bergsaglieri unit. It was Wilbur Wright's 1909 visit to Italy with his demonstration airplane that fired Douhet's imagination and led him to publish his first article on airpower.[42]

Using a naval analogy, Douhet visualized fleets of aircraft that would struggle to achieve "command of the air." To this end he urged the establishment of a military aviation branch; in 1912 he received command of Italy's first aviation unit. This assignment led him into an association with Count Gianni Caproni di Taliedo. Caproni, who had received specialized training in aircraft design at l'Ecole Superieure de Aeronautique et de Construction Mechanique at Liege, was already dreaming up a multiengine bomber. Fired by this vision of long-range bombing, Douhet in 1913 published what was probably the first doctrinal manual for military aviation, *Rules for the Use of Airplanes in War.*[43]

When Douhet proposed a scheme to have Caproni build a fleet of 24 trimotored, 800-horsepower bombers, his superiors, who had greater faith in lighter-than-air dirigibles as vehicles for bombing, turned him down. Undaunted, Douhet then undertook to have Caproni's design developed as an experimental project in the repair shops of his army aviation unit. Upon discovering this subterfuge, the Italian authorities relieved Douhet of his command. The outbreak of World War I, however, gave Caproni the break he needed to go ahead with the development of his bomber. As a result, by 1917 Italy was the only major power with a large long-range, strategic bomber force, having made successful raids on Austrian targets with as many as 250 bombers at a time.[44]

Meanwhile, Douhet, distressed that his superiors were not making better use of airplanes, sent a critical appraisal to one of the government ministries. When his superiors saw the letter, Douhet was court-martialed for slandering the high command and sentenced to a year in prison. While there, he busied himself drafting plans for an inter-Allied air armada similar to the schemes Caproni was urging upon the French and US authorities. After the Italian collapse at Caporetto, Douhet's case was reopened and his criticisms reevaluated; he was restored to duty as director of technical services in the Air Commissariat, from which he retired in 1918.[45]

Up to the time of his retirement, Douhet, if impatient and tactless, had operated within the system. Working in close conjunction with the technically competent Caproni, he [Douhet] advocated doctrinal measures for military aviation that were well within the realm of realism. With retirement, however, came a significant change in Douhet's writings, which became increasingly speculative. His first major work, *Command of the Air*, appearing in 1921 under War Ministry sponsorship, doubtlessly influenced the Italian government in its decision to establish in 1923 an autonomous air ministry with its independent air force, the Aeronautica Regia. In the years that followed, down to his death in 1930, Douhet not only revised his book but turned out a stream of articles in which he prophesied the character of future air war.[46]

Douhet's ideas may be summarized briefly. The air force that achieves command of the air assures a nation of victory. Command of the air must be won by large-scale strategic bombing. The objective of this bombing should not be the enemy military arms but the enemy's ability and will to wage war. This involves bombing factories and cities. Bombing and gassing such civilian targets, Douhet contended, should inflict the maximum damage to materiel and morale in the shortest possible time and thus bring the war to a speedy end. The conventional surface forces, the army and the navy, Douhet reduced to a purely defensive role.[47]

To accomplish command of the air and ultimate victory, Douhet visualized an independent strategic air force using an all-purpose battle plane, a bomber capable of defending itself in the air. He anticipated that such airplanes would be relatively inexpensive to construct and in fact could readily be converted from civilian transports. He even suggested that military pilots could easily be secured from the ranks of commercial pilots by a simple change of uniform.[48] So convinced was Douhet that bombers would be unstoppable and that aggressive offensive operations against the enemy economy would surely carry the day, he even went so far as to suggest that no money should be wasted in building air defenses such as antiaircraft guns.[49]

Although Mussolini's Fascist government found it useful to honor Douhet, it is now clear that his ideas had more value to the Italian authorities as propaganda than as useful doctrinal guides. The Aeronautica Regia never received more than a minor share of the defense budget, and the force structure evolved by Marshal Italo Balbo as air minister certainly did not reflect Douhet's ideas, since most of the planes procured were for tactical use. Douhet claimed that his writings only applied to the special case of Italy; other nations confronted with differing contexts, industrially, geographically, and the like would, he believed, have to modify their application of airpower accordingly. This restrictive caveat is not evident, however, in most of his writings, which tend to be couched in language suggesting general application.[50]

As all present-day readers will recognize, experience in World War II was to show how wrong most of Douhet's speculations actually were. Military pilots, even when drawn from the commercial carriers, required extensive specialized training; civil transport aircraft could not readily be modified for use in combat. Even when bombers were developed fairly bristling with defensive firepower, long-range strategic missions without escort fighters proved to be exceedingly costly. Even when their bomb loads were landed squarely on their assigned targets (which all too often was not the case), the damage inflicted by bomb blast proved to be far less than Douhet had predicted. Cities and their civilian populations proved to be far more resilient than he had anticipated. What is more, the "cheap" weapons he promised failed to materialize as military aircraft costs soared with each technological advance. And finally, in what may have been Douhet's most significant defect, he failed utterly to appreciate that every weapon provokes its own countermeasure.[51]

In short, as long as Douhet remained in uniform and limited his writings to modest projections from the solid ground of experience based on the performance of Caproni bombers, he generated sound doctrine that entitles him to a respected place among the advocates of airpower. But when he retired from service and began writing increasingly speculative pieces with little or no grounding in actual experience, his work became more fanciful and far less useful as doctrinal guidance.

His treatment of what he calls auxiliary aviation—air assets devoted to cooperating with the surface forces—offers a case in point. In his earlier writings on command of the air, he had suggested that the army and navy should be allowed to retain their auxiliary aviation units to assist them in their purely defensive role while the air arm went on the offensive. By 1937, when his revised edition of *Command of the Air* appeared, his unfettered imagination had carried him far beyond this position. Now he confessed he had previously lacked the courage to insist upon the proper course. Now he asserted that all such allocations of air assets to the army and navy diverted needed resources from the air arm and its essential role of achieving mastery of the air—the mission assigned to the independent strategic bombing force he had envisioned. By this line of reasoning, he concluded that to continue the assignment of auxiliary aviation to the army and navy would be "useless, superfluous, and harmful."[52]

When the editors of the French aviation journal *Les Ailes* published a series of articles culminating in a book on Douhet to inject his ideas into the ongoing debate over national defense in France, they invited a number of commentators to put the Italian theorist's notions into context. Most of these writers recognized the significance of Douhet's general proposition that aviation represented a revolution in warfare that would require a rethinking of the whole concept of how combat should be carried out. But they were far less certain when it came to accepting his particular prescriptions. Gen Joseph Tulasne in his foreword reflected this in his comment, "while we may not share all of the ideas of General Douhet, we cannot but help to study them." Another commentator, Etienne Riche, was even more emphatic in warning that Douhet's assertions about abolishing auxiliary aviation should be subjected to close scrutiny: "These efforts must be based on experience, not on any crystallized formulas. Methodical fact finding, tedious study, constantly widening its scope to fit technical possibilities, gives proofs to those who doubt, concrete certainties to who believe."[53]

Here was a sobering reminder that when it came to promulgating sound doctrine, Douhet was a long way behind Moltke. Just as Fuller—for all his brilliance and inventiveness—left no substantial improvement in the way the British military establishment went about devising and perfecting doctrine, so too Douhet seems to have had almost no enduring impact on the Aeronautica Regia and its administrative organization for generating doctrine.

Although Brig Gen William "Billy" Mitchell certainly was not a disciple of Douhet in the sense that Liddell Hart was for Fuller, in many respects his [Mitchell's] career was similar to that of the Italian theorist. Assigned to the General Staff as a Signal Corps captain with no prior experience in aviation, Mitchell was put to work preparing a staff study on the implications of the airplane for the army. This effort sparked his interest in flying. In 1916, when he became deputy to Gen G. O. Squier, who headed the Signal Corps Aviation Section, Mitchell took flying lessons at his own expense. Sent to France as an observer just before the United States entered the war, he was ideally situated to advance his career in aviation. Long talks with Maj Gen Hugh

Trenchard, who headed the air forces of the British Expeditionary Forces, gave him a firm grasp of the doctrinal issues posed by the rapid development of aircraft over the previous three years. One feature of Trenchard's program impressed him particularly. The British had formed a General Headquarters Brigade of aircraft for use in conducting independent strategic operations. To be sure, the limited availability of equipment had kept this force from achieving any very impressive results. The potential was there, however, and later developed into what came to be known as the Independent Force.[54]

Mitchell became an instant convert. Like Douhet, he was convinced from his conversations with Trenchard and numerous other Allied airmen that only a large force of strategic bombers could hope to achieve that superiority in the air that was essential to successful operations on the ground. But when he carried his views back to the headquarters of the American Expeditionary Force, he found little enthusiasm for an independent bomber force.[55] To maintain his credibility within the AEF, Mitchell promptly curbed his outspoken zeal for independent operations and began to concentrate on providing tactical support for Pershing's divisions on the ground. That this was an expedient ploy on his part and did not represent a change of heart is evident from the fact that he continued to correspond with Caproni on the possible procurement of strategic bombers, and at the same time pursued his efforts to assemble target folders on German aircraft factories and other suitable strategic bombing objectives. When the war ended, Mitchell was negotiating with Handley-Page, the British aircraft firm, to procure a force of bombers with a range of no less than 650 miles.[56]

From a personal point of view, Mitchell's decision to mute his advocacy of an independent bombing force in favor of tactical support for the AEF was probably a sound move. Pershing gave him command of the air forces used in the two major AEF assaults, St. Mihiel and Meuse-Argonne, and promoted him to brigadier general. As a consequence, he emerged from the war with the prestige needed to provide him a platform for his postwar advocacy of strategic bombardment.

Mitchell's subsequent career in the service is too well-known to require recapitulation here. The spectacular sinking of the

German battleship *Ostfriesland* tethered in the Chesapeake Bay certainly proved that gravity bombs could sink a naval vessel, but to Billy Mitchell such a conclusion was far too modest. For him the sinking proved that aircraft dominated seacraft. He brushed aside as minor details the fact that the vessel was at anchor and that it was undefended. In a succession of books and articles, he let his imagination soar as he depicted the dominant role of the airplane in the wars of the future.[57]

Mitchell was on solid ground so long as he argued that the traditional services should recognize the revolutionary potential of the airplane and the need for institutional and budgetary adjustments to give substance to this potential. But he was neither systematic nor rigorous in his thinking, and he never developed a carefully thought out doctrine by which the capabilities he claimed for the airplane could be perfected. His forte was publicity. As the hero of the Air Service, AEF, he had a ready-made platform. Unfortunately, his exaggerations, his undisciplined prose, and his tendency to belittle all who disagreed with him induced opposition where he needed cooperation. Naval officers might disagree with his contention that the Navy had been relegated to a secondary position by the airplane, but they could scarcely help being insulted when he claimed that captains and even lieutenants in the air arm had greater responsibilities than admirals in the Navy.[58]

Even before the sinking of the *Ostfriesland,* the admirals of whom Mitchell was so contemptuous had shown that they were by no means blind to the implications of airpower. The General Board had put itself on record on this point:

> There is no doubt that the future employment of aircraft in connection with naval operations will introduce new problems . . . of far-reaching importance. . . . The unlikely may happen and the protective measures and devices needed for the survival of the capital ship may outweigh and overshadow the value of such ships as primary weapons. Before such a condition is reached, however, the new weapons now under trial will have to attain a general efficiency far in excess of anything they now possess. Predictions are one thing, actualities are another. . . . As yet the protected gun is the most generally effective weapon in existence for naval use. But that fact does not relieve us of the necessity of developing to the utmost the new weapons and inventions as rapidly as possible.[59]

Mitchell had little time for such rejoinders. For him the battleship bombings of 1921 and 1923 "clearly demonstrated" the uselessness of expending large sums on the US Navy "where certain superannuated gentlemen known as admirals dictate the practical workings and policies."[60]

After being court-martialed for his intemperate remarks and resigning his commission, Mitchell became even less restrained. So convinced was he that the airplane was the ultimate weapon, that he no longer saw any need for the conventional forces: "We must relegate armies and navies to a place in the glass case of a dusty museum which contains examples of the dinosaur."[61] This kind of rhetorical excess might have been brushed aside as mere verbiage if the general had elsewhere built his doctrinal case with sound factual knowledge, but this he failed to do.

Repeatedly Mitchell made assertions on technical matters without bothering with the necessary underpinning of supporting evidence. For example, he was probably correct in saying that antiaircraft weapons had shown little improvement in the decade since the Armistice, but then he went on to declare: "They never can improve much because a missile-throwing weapon needs a point of reference with which to check the strike of its projectiles. There is no such point in the air." Like Douhet, Mitchell never seemed to consider that countermeasures might be expected to develop just as he anticipated that airplanes would. The inconsistency of his thinking is manifest in the way he reacted to the Navy's adoption of the aircraft carrier, groping its way toward a replacement for the battleship. Aircraft carriers, Mitchell declared, are "useless instruments of war because they are the most vulnerable of all ships under air attack."[62]

Although airpower advocates have found it useful to employ the hero–martyr Mitchell as a symbol, a close study of his writings will quickly reveal the superficiality of his thinking and its lack of solid doctrinal content. It might even be argued that his intemperate style of advocacy did more harm than good to the cause of airpower. The journalist who described him as "the D'Artagnan of the Air" probably had it right.[63] Billy Mitchell was a romantic in an era that called for disciplined analysis in an increasingly complex high-tech field.

In the ongoing struggle to yoke technological advance with appropriate operational doctrine, the role of Sir Henry Tizard offers a revealing contrast to the better-known Billy Mitchell. A World War I pilot who had subsequently become a distinguished leader in the British scientific community, Tizard was to play a pivotal role in the development of Royal Air Force (RAF) fighter doctrine that literally saved the nation during the Battle of Britain.

In the fall of 1934, Dr. Harry E. Wimperis, the director of research for the Air Ministry, appointed Tizard to chair a committee to look into the problem of defense against bombers, a threat just then made more ominously real by Hitler's rapidly expanding Luftwaffe.[64] Just how urgent it was may be suggested by the realization that as late as 1930 the RAF had no monoplane fighters but still relied upon obsolete biplanes so slow they could not overtake a twin-engine Blenheim bomber.[65] When, at the instigation of Wimperis, Dr. Robert Alexander Watson-Watt of the radio department of the National Physical Laboratory brought to the committee a report indicating that there was a distinct possibility that radio waves could be used to locate aircraft in flight, Tizard and his fellow committee members immediately perceived the potential of such an approach. The concept of radio detection was not new; Gulielmo Marconi had suggested its application in detecting ships at sea as far back as 1922. In 1931 the idea had been proposed to the War Office and the Admiralty, but neither had thought well enough of it to find the funds necessary to pursue a development project. Tizard arranged for a crude but effective demonstration by having an airplane fly through the radio waves of a commercial broadcasting station while, on the ground, his committee observed the resulting perturbations on an oscilloscope. Convinced in this way at virtually no cost that the principle was sound, Tizard wheedled a £10,000 grant from the Treasury to press on with further experiments. Undoubtedly his stature as well as the eminence of his committee members, both of whom were fellows of the Royal Society, helped in extracting this vital funding.[66]

Tizard's next step was to approach Air Marshal Hugh Dowding, who then headed RAF Fighter Command after a six-year stint in charge of research at the Air Ministry. It was the great good fortune of Britain that Dowding was an officer with an unusual capacity for objective thinking, a trait he demonstrated repeatedly when making decisions relating to the development of weapon systems.[67] By the spring of 1936, radar devices had been perfected to the point where they could detect planes as much as 75 miles away, but the apparatus was still far from being a useful tactical tool. Accurate determination of altitude still proved elusive. It was at precisely this point that Tizard's significance as a doctrinal thinker became evident.[68]

As chairman of a scientific advisory committee, Tizard could easily have assumed that his role was to see to it that potentially useful ideas were brought to the attention of the service authorities. His vision went further, however. As he spelled out in a memo in 1936, the advisory committee had two tasks. One was to help in the development of the technology that would perform the desired function; the other was to work with the appropriate service branch to ensure that the apparatus, when developed, was adequately integrated into the tactical doctrine of the operating units. To this end he urged that arrangements be made to ensure the cooperation of the major RAF operating commands to secure their constructive criticism.[69]

In August 1936, Tizard arranged for an extended test of radar at RAF Biggin Hill. In this undertaking he demonstrated his remarkable grasp of the many pitfalls that beset the operational testing of a technological innovation. One can only surmise that this awareness stemmed from his earlier experience as a test pilot assigned to the RAF development center at Farnborough during World War I. To begin with, he was at great pains to select only the most open-minded and promising RAF officers to participate in the tests. That he was an excellent judge of men is suggested by the fact that nearly all the officers he chose eventually rose to high rank in the RAF.[70]

Tizard understood that the outcome of any test can be substantially determined by the way in which its sponsors design the process of evaluation. To avoid this kind of bias, he assembled the officers who were to participate in the experiment and, without disclosing the apparatus they were to test, he described its capabilities as if they were merely hypothetical and then asked them to explain how they would go about planning to use such a device to intercept incoming enemy aircraft. In this way he elicited their best creative responses. Not surprisingly, when the various schemes of interception were actually tried in the air, all sorts of difficulties arose.

Tizard showed his deep understanding of the human dimensions in his task when he criticized Watson-Watt for proposing tests that were certain to result in failure. Disheartening results, he pointed out, could readily so prejudice the air officers concerned that they might be induced to terminate the experiment before it achieved persuasive results. To avoid this danger of throwing out the baby with the bath water, Tizard envisioned the need to stage a carefully graded set of trials that made possible steady improvement by means of modifications in tactics and in the design of the apparatus itself. By the end of two months of such prudently escalated trials, the RAF pilots were making successful intercepts in 85 percent of their sorties. On this evidence, Dowding, now fully persuaded that he had a revolutionary new weapon at his disposal, arranged to have construction begun on a series of radar stations covering the eastern and southern approaches to the United Kingdom. But even then, the new weapon was far from operationally complete.[71]

The final step in converting radar from a scientific toy to a fully functional weapon system was largely the work of Dowding of Fighter Command. It was he who presided over the creation of a command-and-control system with its filter centers and plot boards all linked to the coastal radar stations by a redundant series of communication lines. By the summer of 1937 the system had been substantially perfected. Standardized terminology was worked out so that pilots in the air and controllers on the ground could function smoothly as a team, the whole converging at Bentley Priory, Fighter Command headquarters. As a consequence, when war came in 1939, "the few"—to whom so many owed so much—were ready.[72]

Tizard's name has never become a household word in the sense that Billy Mitchell's has, but in the business of developing the doctrinal process it seems clear that he contributed far more than his better-known predecessor. While it is certainly true that he deserves much credit for his role in developing radar, it was not the basic electronic theory that gave the

British such a decided edge over the enemy. After all, the Germans also had radar that they were developing more or less in parallel with the RAF. The big difference came from the fact that the British pushed farther. They not only deployed radar as a weapon system but also devised sound tactical doctrine to guide its use and provided the operational training needed to ensure that the system actually functioned in practice. In all of this, Tizard played a dominant role.[73]

Tizard's contributions to the doctrinal process can be summarized briefly. It was he who showed the importance of establishing a close working relationship between the scientists on one hand and the military services on the other.[74] This has become such a commonplace in the post-World War II era that it is sometimes difficult to recall just how alien the two professions were earlier. Moreover, Tizard's initiatives gave a significant impetus to the kind of scientific analysis of weapon systems which has come to be called operational research or OR.[75] Ironically, soon after he performed his nation-saving services he was maneuvered out of his position by political machinations and spent the rest of the war somewhat on the sidelines. This fate also befell his collaborator Air Marshal Dowding.[76]

What insights can we derive from the brief survey of the several doctrinal thinkers presented here? Congreve came up with a brilliant conceptualization of the doctrinal problem, limited to be sure, but nonetheless a remarkably imaginative beginning. He failed, however, to institutionalize his contribution, and for more than a hundred years afterward the British lacked an effective system for perfecting military doctrine that would cope with the stream of technological innovations in weaponry churned up by the industrial revolution.[77]

Notes

1. Robert A. Doughty, *The Seeds of Disaster: The Development of French Army Doctrine, 1919–1939* (Hamden, Conn.: Archon Books, 1985), 184; and Barry R. Posen, *The Sources of Military Doctrine* (Ithaca, N.Y.: Cornell University Press, 1984), 113–14.

2. Doughty, 188.

3. Ferdinand 0. Miksche, *Attack: A Study in Blitzkrieg Tactics* (New York: Random House, 1912), 7.

4. Doughty, 2.

5. I. B. Holley Jr., "The Doctrinal Process," *Military Review* 59 (April 1979): 2–13.

6. Carl von Clausewitz, *On War*, trans. and ed. Michael Howard and Peter Paret (Princeton, N.J.: Princeton University Press, 1976), 127.

7. B. H. Liddell Hart, *Strategy* (New York: Praeger, 1951), 353.

8. Ralph Sanders, "Technology and Strategy: A Realistic Assessment," *Technology in Society* 5, no. 2 (1983): 141–42; and Michael Howard, *Studies in War and Peace* (London: Temple Smith, 1959), 34.

9. William Congreve, *The Details of the Rocket System* [short title, see narrative for full title], reprint of the original edition, London: Whiting, 1814 (Ottawa, Canada: Museum Restoration Service, 1970), 7–8.

10. See biographical sketch of Congreve in *Dictionary of National Biography* (Oxford: Oxford University Press, 1921–1922), vol. 4, as well as *Encyclopedia Britannica* 1985 ed., s. v. "Congreve." Biographical sketch by Frank H. Winter in Charles C. Gillispie, ed., *Dictionary of Scientific Biography* (New York: Scribners, 1971); and Winter, "Sir William Congreve, 1771–1828" in Ernst A. Steinhoff, ed., *The Eagle Has Returned*, pt. 11, published as a supplement, "Advances in Astronautical Sciences," *Science and Technology* 45 (1977): 224–37, a publication of the American Astronautical Society. The documentation for this article offers an extensive bibliography on Congreve.

11. Congreve, 10–11.

12. Robert Scales, "Artillery in Small Wars: The Evolution of British Artillery Doctrine, 1860–1914" (unpublished dissertation, Department of History, Duke University, Durham, N.C.: 1976). For Liddell Hart's several abortive efforts to establish an appropriate operational research organization for the British Army, see Gen Sir Frederick Pile's chapter, "Liddell Hart and the British Army, 1919–1939," in Michael Howard, *Theory and Practice of War* (N.Y.: Praeger, 1966), 176–78.

13. Walter Gorlitz, *History of the German General Staff* (London: Hollis-Carter, 1953), 69–75; W. O. C. Morris, *Moltke: A Biographical and Critical Study* (London: Ward and Downey, 1894); and Frederick E. Whitton, *Moltke* (London: Constable, 1921) for biographical details on Helmuth von Moltke.

14. Whitton, 24–68; Gorlitz, 71.

15. Charles Edward White, *The Enlightened Soldier: Scharnhorst and the Militarische Gesellschaft* (New York: Praeger, 1989), 49–58.

16. *Handbüch der Artillerie* (Hanover: 1804–1814), quoted in Peter Paret, *Yorck and the Era of Prussian Reform: 1807–1814* (Princeton, N.J.: Princeton University Press, 1966), 119.

17. J. F. C. Fuller, *Armament and History* (New York: Scribner, 1945), 116–17.

18. Dennis Showalter, *Railroads and Rifles: Soldiers, Technology and the Unification of Germany* (Hamden, Conn.: Shoestring Press, 1975), 111; and Whitton, 73–75.

19. Morris, 39–42.

20. Dallas Irvine, "The French and Prussian Staff Systems before 1870," *Journal of the American Military Foundation* [JAAAF] 2 (Winter 1938): 195. The JAAAF is now the *Journal of Military History*.

21. Gorlitz, 77; Showalter, 113–15; Whitton, 71.

22. Martin L. van Creveld, *Command in War* (Cambridge: Harvard University Press, 1985), 108.

23. Ibid., 124.

24. Edwin A. Pratt, *The Rise of Rail Power in War and Conquest, 1833–1914* (London: P. S. King, 1916), 104.

25. Showalter, 50.

26. Pratt, 105.

27. Irvine, 196; and Gerhard Ritter, *The Sword and the Scepter* (Coral Gables, Fla.: University of Florida Press, 1969), 1, 185.

28. Pratt, 106. See also Rudoph von Cammerer, *The Development of Strategical Science* (London: Hugh Reeves, 1905), translation from the German edition.

29. Jay Luvaas, *Education of an Army: British Military Thought, 1815–1940* (Chicago: University of Chicago Press, 1964), 336ff; Basil H. Liddell Hart, *The Tanks*, vol. 1 (New York: Praeger, 1959), 120–21.

30. J. F. C. Fuller, *Memoirs of an Unconventional Soldier* (London: Nicholson and Watson, 1936), 320.

31. Fuller, *Memoirs*, 323–25.

32. Ibid., 3–17.

33. Fuller, *Armament and History*, 18.

34. Anthony J. Trythal, *"Boney" Fuller* (New Brunswick, N.J.: Rutgers University Press, 1977), 80.

35. Royal United Service Institution (RUSI) *Journal* 65 (May 1920): 239.

36. Ibid., 247.

37. Ibid., 261.

38. Ibid., 260.

39. Robin Higham, *The Military Intellectuals in Britain, 1918–1939* (New Brunswick, N.J.: Rutgers University Press, 1966), 44.

40. Luvaas, 371–74, 387, 409; and Robert O'Neill, "Doctrine and Training in the German Army" in Michael Howard, *Theory and Practice*, 145ff.

41. Basil H. Liddell Hart, *The Liddell Hart Memoirs* (New York: Putnam, 1956), I: 229.

42. For brief biographical sketches, see Jean Romeyer, "Giulio Douhet," in *Air Warfare* (Washington, D.C.: Office Chief of Air Corps, 12 November 1933), 6, a mimeographed translation from the French aviation journal *L'Ailes;* and *Encyclopedia Italiana*, Appendix A-H (Treves: Instituto G. Treecani, 1938), 527. See also William H. Tomlinson, "The Father of Air Power Doctrine," *Military Review* 46 (September 1966): 27–28.

43. Boone Atkinson, "The Caproni Museum and Archives," *Airpower Historian* (October 1957), 186; and Tomlinson, 28. On Caproni, see Giovanni Battista Gianni, *Dictionaria Biografice Degli Italiano* (Rome: Instituto Della Enciclopedia Italiana, 1976).

44. Atkinson, "Italian Influence on the Origins of the American Concept of Strategic Bombardment," *Airpower Historian* (July 1957), 142; and *Enciclopedia Italiana*, Appendix, 1938 ed., s. v. *"Guerra."*

45. Tomlinson, 28–29; and Atkinson, "Italian Influence,"144.

46. Giulio Douhet, *Command of the Air* (Washington, D.C.: 1983), a reprint by the Office of Air Force History of the 1942 translation published by Coward-McCann, New York.

47. William D. Franklin, "Douhet Revisited," *Military Review* 47 (November 1967): 65–69, offers a brief review of Douhet's ideas as does Edward Warner in Edward M. Earle, *Makers of Modern Strategy* (Princeton: Princeton University Press, 1943), chap. 20.

48. *Air Warfare*, 41–42.

49. Alfred Hurley, *Billy Mitchell* (Bloomington, Ind.: Indiana University Press, 1975), 114.

50. Claudio G. Segre, "Douhet in Italy: Prophet Without Honor," *Aerospace Historian* (June 1979), 69–80.

51. Earle, 493–94. See also "The Heritage of Douhet," in Bernard Brodie, *Strategy in the Missile Age* (Princeton, N.J.: Princeton University Press, 1960).

52. Romeyer, 8.

53. Ibid., 2. See also unnumbered introductory pages by Etienne Riche as well as Col Arsene M. P. Vautier in *La Doctrine de Guerre de General Douhet* (Paris: Berger-Levrault, 1935).

54. Hurley, 15, 25–26.

55. On opposition to strategic bombing, see Col Edgar S. Gorrell, "An American Proposal for Strategic Bombing in World War I," *Aerospace Historian* 5 (April 1958): 114–17.

56. Atkinson, "Caproni Museum," 32.

57. William L. Mitchell, *Winged Defense* (New York: Putnam, 1925), 56.

58. Ibid., xviii.

59. Lt Comdr Lee P. Warren, "The Battleship Still Supreme," *World's Week* 41 (April 1921): 556–59.

60. William L. Mitchell, "Building a Futile Navy," *Atlantic Monthly* 142 (September 1928): 409–10.

61. William L. Mitchell, "Airplanes in National Defense," American Academy of Political Science *Annals* 131 (May 1927): 12.

62. Mitchell, "Building," 411–12.

63. N. S. Waterhouse, "D'Artagnan of the Air," *Christian Science Monitor,* 9 October 1935, 5.

64. J. G. Crowther and R. Widdington, *Science at War* (New York: Philosophical Library, 1948), 3–4.

65. Peter Wykeham, *Fighter Command* (London: Putnam, 1960), 54.

66. Ronald W. Clark, *Tizard* (Cambridge, Mass.: MIT Press, 1965), 113–17. The other two members were P. M. S. Blackett and A. V. Hill.

67. Basil Collier, *Leader of the Few* (London: Jarrolds, 1957), 146, 202.

68. Clark, 130.

69. Ibid., 135.

70. Ibid., 155–56.

71. Crowther, 10; and Clark, 153–54.

72. Robert Wright, *The Man Who Won the Battle of Britain* (New York: Scribner, 1969), 63.

73. P. M. S. Blackett, *Studies of War: Nuclear and Conventional* (Edinburgh: Oliver and Boyd, 1962), 101–110; and Blackett, "Tizard and the Science of War," *Scientific American* 204 (April 1961): 191.

74. James P. Baxter, *Scientists Against Time* (Boston: Little Brown, 1946), 122.

75. Blackett, *Studies of War,* 101–103. For the political machinations of Lord Cherwell, Viscount F. A. Lindemann, "the Prof," to push Tizard aside, see Clark, 121; Blackett, 204; and Clark, 191ff.

76. For the political maneuvering that led to the ousting of Dowding, see Wright, 205–10.

77. I am indebted to my colleague Professor Alex Roland for constructive criticism of this paper and to Frank H. Winter and Walter J. Boyne of the National Air and Space Museum for providing a wealth of material on Sir William Congreve.

THIS PAGE INTENTIONALLY LEFT BLANK

Essay 5

Weapons and Doctrine:
A Historical Introduction*

An English army of several thousand men led by a renowned officer landed on the coast of Normandy and pressed eastward in a raiding expedition penetrating almost to Paris. The officer was Edward III, king of England—the time, July 1346. However remote the day—now more than 600 years past, the expedition is still worthy of study for its military lessons.

Edward's troopers loitered and plundered along the way until they were suddenly confronted with a French host hurriedly gathered to resist their advance. The spot was not a strategic one for battle. Since the fleet of convoys that had carried the English army across the Channel had returned home, retreat along the path of advance was impossible. The only alternative to fighting was withdrawal toward Flanders. Crossing the Seine near Paris, the English made for the Somme, but here they found the crossings guarded as they tried the fords one after another down the length of the river. At last, with some difficulty the whole English force managed to slip across the salt flats below Abbeville just ahead of the flood tide, which prevented French pursuit for a full 12 hours. With the period of grace thus secured, Edward led his troops through the forest of Crécy and at leisure selected a defensive position with the wood at his back and a long gentle downward slope of open ground before him. Here, on a site of his own choosing, the king drew up his men in battle array—three great blocks or *batailles* of dismounted knights and men-at-arms with connecting ranks of archers armed with English longbows.

---

*This piece appeared originally as the first chapter in the author's book *Ideas and Weapons*, which has appeared in four different editions, first in 1953 (Yale University Press), then in 1971 (Archon), and 1983 (Government Printing Office, [GPO]). The GPO edition was reprinted in a paperback version in 1997. It offers numerous historical examples of the interrelationship of technological advance and the development of doctrine, ranging from the Middle Ages to the recent past.

The French forces under King Philip of Valois approached this position in a disorder that reflected both the speed of pursuit and the confusion of a hurried river crossing. Against the French king's wishes, the rash and undisciplined feudal lords assailed the English position. Each new group of Frenchmen to arrive on the scene thrust forward in attack, and without exception each suffered the same fate. The English archers with their longbows stopped the drive before the French could fairly engage the standing men-at-arms and dismounted knights.

Medieval chronicles are notoriously unreliable when dealing with numbers. However, even if one rejects Jean Froissart's figures, the evidence still indicates that the English won the Battle of Crécy with a force approximately half that of the French; and, with so markedly inferior a force, the English archers ended the long supremacy of feudal cavalry. If the French dead in this battle (more than 1,500 "lords and knights" on the field of Crécy) were not enough to spell out the revolution achieved by the longbow, later events in the Hundred Years' War, when the French learned to dread the English arrow, made the implications of the new weapon only too clear.[1] Sir Charles Oman says the fight at Crécy was "a revelation to the Western World," a startling demonstration of the supremacy of the longbow over the armored knight on horseback.

One would assume that the English kings must have been seeking eagerly to counterbalance their country's inevitable numerical inferiority with such a weapon as had wrought this revolution in arms. On the contrary, the longbow appears to have been on the English back doorstep for nearly 250 years before Crécy. English warfare from the time of the Norman invasion to Edward I—1066 to 1277—was of two sorts: continental wars in which mailed horsemen did the principal fighting and infantry were of little concern, and local wars with the Irish and Welsh. A Welsh historian, Giraldus Cambrensis, whose *Expugnatio* appeared sometime in the middle of the twelfth century, wrote at length on the Welsh use of the longbow in the border wars and recommended an increase in the number of Welsh archers in the Anglo-Norman armies to enhance their firepower.[2] Like the advice of many military historians, this proposal appears to have gone unheeded.

The bow, of course, had long been known in England. Archers armed with the short bow, known since Roman times, had participated in the fray at Hastings. But the insignificance of the bow is revealed by the absence of any mention of it in the Assize of Arms held by Henry II in 1181. By the time of the next assize in 1252 during the reign of Henry III, the influence of the Welsh had become apparent; citizens with 40-shilling holdings or less were required to appear at the muster armed with the longbow. During the Welsh and Scottish border wars of the thirteenth century, Edward I perfected the use of the longbow in conjunction with cavalry until finally in 1298, at the Battle of Falkirk, the English, using longbows, demolished a Scots force under William Wallace.

Unfortunately, English chroniclers in recording the battle "forgot that the archers had prepared the way, and only remembered the victorious charge of the knights at the end of the day."[3] The importance of comprehensive tactical analysis was unrecognized, and Edward's lesson was lost when the king died in 1306 without leaving a written record of his military art. When the Scots under Robert Bruce put Edward's son and his English army to rout at the Battle of Bannockburn in 1314 by using a judicious combination of cavalry and longbowmen, Bruce proved himself the abler pupil of Edward I. The training acquired in continual border wars enabled Edward III to lead to Crécy an army skilled in the use of the longbow, which worked such havoc among the "fiery and undisciplined noblesse" of the French.

Oman finds it "rather surprising" that Edward III was so slow in heeding the "obvious" lesson of the preponderant influence of the longbow and increasing the proportion of bowmen in his forces.[4] How much more surprising is the painfully slow advance of the longbow as an English weapon. There are nearly 250 years between Cambrensis's advocacy of the Welsh elm bow and Crécy; yet the lesson of the border wars was plain: a new weapon gave one side an advantage over the other. Crécy is chosen to illustrate this principle because the battle took place more than 600 years ago and is sufficiently remote to be free from all interests, prejudices, and emotions that surround so many present military practices.

57

Other examples are plentiful. In 479 B.C. at the Battle of Plataea, the Persian rabble fled in dismay before Greeks using an innovation in warfare, which consisted of a phalanx of troops marching in step with shields aligned—in truth, a mobile armored force.[5] In the spring of 1940 a handful of British fighters broke the back of the German aerial invasion because they had an innovation called radar.

Sometimes the advantage of a superior weapon is decisive before countermeasures can be evolved. It follows then that the methods used to select and develop new weapons and the doctrines concerning their use will have an important bearing upon the success or failure of armies—and of nations. A brief résumé of some of the more important developments in weapons and the circumstances surrounding their adoption in the United States should provide an adequate perspective for the narrower problem, which is the subject of this study. One need go no further back than the nineteenth century.

Consider, for instance, the annual report of Joel R. Poinsett, secretary of war in 1840, which discussed at length the problem of introducing new weapons. After reviewing a number of projects undertaken by the Ordnance Department, the secretary declared that the necessities of national security generally inclined him "to discountenance" all "new inventions" unless convinced of their superiority "by long-tried experiments in the field." In the matter of breech-loading weapons, the secretary was emphatic: "I fear that every attempt . . . will fail as they have hitherto done, after involving the government in great expense." On the other hand, the percussion cap for flintlock muskets found official favor inasmuch as this particular innovation had been "fairly tested in the field by the armies of Europe."[6] The policy of the War Department, it appears, was to follow, not lead. When a patent breech-loading carbine was offered to the department in 1842, the colonel of ordnance agreed to a trial of the new weapon but noted that it was not customary for the government to incur any expense beyond the consumption of ammunition. The colonel was quick to point out that not all the fault lay with Ordnance: "A prejudice against all arms loading at the breech is prevalent among officers, and especially the Dragoons." Moreover, the colonel doubted that the new breechloader could be introduced into the service even if it were found to be better than other models.[7]

Between 1842 and 1845 the Ordnance Department conducted a number of tests on breech-loading weapons. The results were extremely discouraging, as might be expected of a new technological process in the testing stage. The colonel of ordnance, an official whose status might be fairly translated as chief of ordnance in later times, reported on the problem to the secretary of war: "Upon due consideration of the subject the department decided on abandoning the manufacture of breech-loading arms, and have followed in the steps of the great powers of Europe, deciding that a diversity of arms was productive of evil, and adopting those of ordinary construction which are the simplest and easiest managed by the common soldier." So firmly convinced of the virtues of muzzle-loading muskets of "ordinary construction" was this colorful colonel that he put himself on record concerning the soon-to-be-famous Colt's patent arms: "That they will ultimately all pass into oblivion cannot be doubted." Meanwhile, he warned, it would be well for officers to take care not to be "ensnared again by the projects of inventors."[8]

The patent carbine that the colonel of ordnance found so undesirable was able to fire more than 14,000 rounds before it broke down in proving trials. Unfortunately a service test with troops in the field was hard to obtain. The company officer to whom the carbines were issued must have been a dragoon; he replied, when pressed for a report on service tests, that the carbines were not worth the storeroom they occupied.[9] A hundred years later, procedures for following up service tests were still a troublesome matter.

When summarizing the whole problem of breechloaders in 1851, a subsequent chief of ordnance made it clear that his department was not utterly blind to the innovation. He admitted the real advantage of breech-loading weapons but indicated that these advantages were difficult if not impossible to obtain without sacrificing the essential qualities of simplicity and durability. The department would continue to use muzzleloaders until it encountered "convincing proof" of superior breechloaders.[10] Here then was a step forward. The chief of ordnance recognized the validity of the principle of breech loading and differentiated between the principle as an objective sought and individual inventions that failed, for mechanical or technical reasons, to satisfy the requirements of the principle. His view represented a marked advance over the attitude of the previous colonel of ordnance who had summarily rejected the principle of breech-loading weapons merely because repeated attempts at application had ended in failure.

By 1859 war and the rumor of war had worked a real change in the Ordnance Department, which now professed to "encourage the application of scientific knowledge and mechanical skill to improvements in arms." The department was on the verge of adopting a breech-loading carbine, but "uniformity of armament" was so obviously essential for training and for supply of ammunition in time of war that ordnance officials were reluctant to issue any one new type before deciding upon the best. The final selection, it was pointed out, might well fall upon an arm "not yet invented."[11] This desire for the utmost qualitative superiority was admirable, but with open rebellion a few months off, the time for decisions on what to produce was already at hand, even if it was a weapon somewhat short of the ideal. Secretary of War John B. Floyd was certainly not unaware of the potentialities of breechloaders. After reviewing the "wonderfully numerous" experiments with the innovation, he considered them "by far the most efficient arms ever put into the hands of intelligent men" and recommended that immediate steps be taken to arm all light troops with breechloaders. To do less, he declared, was "an inhuman economy."[12] Unfortunately for the Federal cause, in this respect at least, Secretary Floyd "went South," and the Ordnance Department continued to seek the best breechloaders but not to issue them.

As late as February 1861, the colonel of ordnance declared that the muzzle-loader of the service was "unsurpassed for military purposes." And the value of repeating arms was curtly dismissed by the colonel, who pointed out that they had been known to misfire and that front-rank men would be "more in dread of those behind than of the enemy." That repeating arms would do away with the tactical maneuver of multiple ranks attacking in close order across open ground seems never to have occurred to this officer. His was by no means an isolated expression of opinion. At about the same time another ordnance officer said of the musket issued by the United States that there is "no superior arm in the world," an opinion he was willing to back by proposing that the Ordnance Department absolutely refuse to answer any requisitions for new and untried arms.[13]

By 1864 the pressure of wartime operations had changed a great many opinions and led to the replacement of several key officers in the Ordnance Department. The new officials accelerated the pace of experiment, and both breechloaders and repeating arms were issued in relatively small quantities to troops in the field for service tests. While lamenting the difficulties of securing accurate reports from the troops on the merits or demerits of any given weapon, the new chief of ordnance reported that urgent demands from the field left no doubt that repeating arms were the favorite of the army.[14] Similarly, Secretary of War E. M. Stanton was informed that breech-loading weapons were now "greatly superior" to the musket manufactured by the national armories and that the time had come to decide upon a breechloader for issue to the service. The moment was in December 1865.[15]

To assume that the adoption of breechloaders must be a simple matter, once official opinion lined up behind the project, would be naïve. There is a great difference between the giving of an order and its actual execution in every detail. In 1867 when the war was safely in the background, a joint congressional committee on ordnance presented a resolution to stop the modification of service muskets into breechloaders since such modification would render useless existing stocks of ammunition."[16] Reasons of economy no doubt motivated this congressional interference in a technical decision. Congress might well have interfered sooner, for there were more than a million obsolete muskets unissued at the end of the war.[17]

The well-known British military critic and student of war, B. H. Liddell Hart, in commenting on the Union and Confederate armies, credits the few repeating arms that actually reached the hands of Federal troops in action with a "decisive influence" out of all proportion to their numbers. He bolsters his contention by quoting Confederate Gen E. P. Alexander to the effect that the war might have been terminated within one year if the Federal infantry had been equipped with even the imperfect repeaters of 1861 design.[18] Liddell Hart makes a point of exceptional importance. In spite of the high quality of generalship exhibited in the war, armament lagged "well behind the pace of invention." But more important than the hither edge of invention, which sometimes lies beyond the scope of production, was the failure to utilize new weapons that were not only technically possible but also capable of being produced on an extensive scale.

F. A. Shannon, the author of a classic study on the Union army, makes the same point even more forcibly. The North, with its control of the seas and adequate industry, was free to choose the weapons it wanted. Unfortunately, the North's choice was not the best weapon available but a musket modified since the Revolution by little more than the addition of the percussion lock and rifling. Thus, the North fought with the same weapons available to the South and made slight use of the superior arms within its grasp. Shannon considers it a strange paradox that the North used every means, including bribery, to increase its firepower by pressing more and more men into the ranks and at the same time failed, until late in the war, to increase firepower by putting better weapons in the hands of the trained men already in the ranks.[19] Eighty-odd years later the problem of correlating technological advance in weapons with higher national policy was still far from being entirely solved.

If armies have been slow in applying the maxim that superior arms favor victory, it may be shown that their intransigence has resulted to a great extent from three specific shortcomings in the procedure for developing new weapons. These shortcomings appear to have been a failure to adopt, actively and positively, the thesis that superior arms favor victory; a failure to recognize the importance of establishing a doctrine regarding the use of weapons; and a failure to devise effective techniques for recognizing and evaluating potential weapons in the advances of science and technology.

Although military men have been slow to recognize and put into practice the thesis that superior arms favor victory, military writers down through the ages have given some recognition to the importance of weapons. Vegetius* in his *Military Institu-tions,* which has been aptly described as the field service man-ual of the Imperial Roman Army, recognized the relative im-portance of materiel. "The Legion," said Vegetius, "owes its success to its arms and machines, as well as to the number and bravery of its soldiers."[20] Authorities can be found repeat-ing the truism in every century down to our own, pointing out that fighting soon led men to special inventions that they turned to their advantage.[21] Yet a decided disparity has pre-vailed between frequent assertion of the thesis that inventions could be put to military advantage and the paucity of studies on the application of the thesis in practical terms. Most mili-tary writers have bowed obsequiously in the general direction of the principle, but having done this they rush on to the sup-posedly more important subjects of strategy and command. Sometimes tactics are treated with attention to detail, but weapons have generally been dismissed with the slighting treat-ment combat soldiers usually reserve for rear-echelon supply troops. A bare handful of writers has specialized in the problem of weapons; almost all others, dealing more generally with war-fare, have either relegated the subject to a minor position or ig-nored it entirely.[22]

The great Carl von Clausewitz, who dominated military think-ing for nearly a hundred years following the demise of the Napoleonic Empire, admitted in *Vom Krieg* that superiority in the organization and equipment of an army has at times given "a great moral preponderance," but having made this concession he points out how clear it must be that "arming and equipping are not essential to the conception of fighting." Even while conceding that fighting determined the character of arms and that arms modified the character of war, Clausewitz restricted the "art" of war, by entirely arbitrary definition, to the actual conduct of bat-tle. To include the problems of arms and equipment, he said, would be to establish a special case rather than a timeless prin-ciple.[23] Unlike Adam Smith, Clausewitz wrote after the Industrial Revolution was well under way, but his writings show an utter lack of appreciation of the implications for the development of

---

*Flavius Vegetius Renatus

weapons in the new mechanization. Just how static Clausewitz's concept of the evolution of weapons was is shown in his contention that "completing and replacing articles of arms and equipment . . . takes place only periodically, and therefore seldom affects strategic plans."[24] Weapons, it would appear, were taken for granted by the military theorists of the nineteenth century. Baron Antoine Henri de Jomini, who was perhaps the leading military theorist of that century next to Clausewitz, made a concession to materiel in granting extensive consideration to logistics; yet even he defined logistics in the former sense of "the practical art of moving armies" rather than in the broader contemporary definition, which embraces more of the element of production.[25]

The myopia demonstrated by these theorists had a profound influence upon those military leaders who dominated the profession of arms down to World War I. Gen Ferdinand Foch, when he published his *Principles of War* in 1903, carried on in the tradition of Clausewitz. His "principles" concerned strategy and tactics (or the use of weapons). The selection, development, and procurement of superior weapons he ignored or assumed. When Foch at length came to dominate the councils of both France and the Allies, his emphasis on personnel rather than materiel helped determine the character of the armies that fought in World War I.[26] The absurdities created by the failure to emphasize the importance of superiority in weapons in the years leading up to 1914 were nowhere more vividly portrayed than in France. In the nation of the mass army, Gen F. G. Herr reported the prevailing attitude: "The battle will be primarily a struggle between two infantries, where victory will rest with the large battalions; the army must be an army of personnel and not of materiel."[27] This attitude probably marked the apogee of neglect for the thesis of superior weapons.

The events of World War I abruptly focused attention upon the relative significance of materiel in securing victory. The Italian general Giulio Douhet, philosopher of airpower, expressed the new emphasis on materiel when he said, "The form of any war . . . depends upon the technical means of war available."[28] Douhet was, of course, a theorist whose writings could be said to represent little more than his own personal opinions; the writings of the Americans Benedict Crowell and William Crozier on the new importance of industry and weapons in modern warfare were more significant as indices of the new trend.[29] World War I awakened in military circles a new realization of the importance of weapons, but the emphasis was on quantity rather than quality. The first postwar report by the secretary of war emphasized the need for a broader scope of training for military men. New weapons and new methods of warfare, the secretary said, made it "specially apparent" that staff officers should have not only a wider knowledge of their purely military duties but also a "full comprehension of all agencies, governmental as well as industrial, necessarily involved in a nation at war."[30]

This new awareness of the importance of industry received positive expression in the postwar provisions made for the planning of industrial mobilization and in the formation of the Army Industrial College to train officers in its techniques.[31] But materiel alone did not signify superiority of weapons: planning for industrial mobilization emphasized quantitative procurement—more weapons rather than better weapons. To be sure, centers for research and development and the millions devoted to improving weapons during this period show that the concept of superior weapons was not entirely neglected between the two world wars. Nevertheless, it was not until World War II and the approach of total war that military men and governments generally accepted and implemented the thesis of superior weapons as a cardinal tenet of military policy.[32]

To carry the résumé of changing attitudes toward the thesis that superior weapons favor victory down through World War II would be to go beyond the scope of this study. The brief review already presented is useful, nevertheless, in that it makes more understandable the comparative paucity of interest and attention that the military men have until recently devoted to the problem of revising doctrine to embrace new weapons. Without a tradition of positive and active adherence to this thesis as a prior condition, it is not surprising that the problem of relating doctrine to technological advance in weapons received only belated attention—in most instances long after the weapon itself had become available.

Superiority in weapons stems not only from a selection of the best ideas from advancing technology but also from a system that relates the ideas selected to a doctrine or concept of their tactical or strategic application, which is to say the accepted concept of the mission to be performed by any given weapon. Protracted and serious delays in the adoption of superior weapons have led critics to charge military men with congenital conservatism.[33] But it sometimes has happened that new weapons have been developed, adopted as standard, issued, and then neglected for lack of accepted doctrine regarding their use. It has probably more often happened that new weapons have been adopted and even used to a certain extent but that their full potential value has remained unexploited because higher policy-making echelons have failed to modify prevailing doctrine to embrace the innovation. New weapons when not accompanied by correspondingly new adjustments in doctrine are just so many external accretions on the body of an army.

Liddell Hart cites the case of Capt Émile Mayer of the French army. A contemporary of Foch and Joseph-Jacques-Césaire Joffre at the École Polytechnique, Mayer accepted a position as military editor for the *Revue scientifique* where he became aware of the impact of military invention on doctrine. His prolific writings developed the thesis that new ideas—smokeless powder, for example—demanded new doctrines of war. Unfortunately, the revised doctrines he advocated did not jibe with prevailing French military policy. Mayer was retired as a captain long before his contemporaries who were more willing to conform to accepted doctrines.[34] The incident is noteworthy only insofar as it serves to emphasize the difficulties involved in attempting to modify existing military thought. To introduce radical changes in the doctrines of warfare is to run headlong into the opposition of the entrenched interests. The bowyers' and fletchers' guilds were probably mortal enemies of the advocates of gunpowder. The belated demise of cavalry in the United States during 1946 and the anachronistic survival of captive balloons for the purpose of observation until the eve of World War II give some indication of the obstinate resistance of military institutions to doctrinal changes. But for all of this, the greatest stumbling block to the revision of doctrine was probably not so much vested interests as the absence of a system for analyzing new weapons and their relation to prevailing concepts of utilizing weapons.

"Victory smiles upon those who anticipate changes in the character of war," Douhet wrote, "not upon those who wait to adapt themselves after the changes occur."[35] Unfortunately military men have had difficulty in providing the means of anticipating changes. Gen J. F. C. Fuller, one of the most prolific of British writers on warfare, may be unduly harsh when he says "soldiers are mostly alchemists;" but he is probably correct in attributing the difficulty to a lack of scientific method in analyzing the elements comprising the revolutionary changes that have modified the character of warfare.[36] To go further into the reasons why armies have been slow in adjusting doctrine to advances in weapons would be to digress needlessly. Here it is important only to recognize the implications of this shortcoming. The events surrounding the development of doctrine for three well-known weapons will serve to illustrate the point that to adopt a new weapon without a new doctrine is to throw away advantage.

The machine-gun was no new invention in 1914. As early as 1885 the modern machine-gun was known in the United States. Even though the weapon had not yet emerged from the experimental stage, the chief of ordnance predicted then that it would in the future become "a prominent factor in every contest."[37] Some years later, during the Russo-Japanese War of 1905, British observers reported that machine-guns were working a "great execution."[38] But the experience of the Russo-Japanese War had no influence on British military doctrine as far as machine-guns were concerned. Before the observers reported on the startling effectiveness of the novel weapon in actual warfare there were 24 machine-guns in each British division or two per battalion. In 1914 the machine-gun strength of each division was exactly what it had been in 1899. In view of the scale of expenditures for other types of weapons during this period, it must certainly have been military policy and not limited appropriations that determined the number of machine-guns authorized. By the end of 1918 there were more than 500 machine-guns in each British division.[39] The increase represented a revolution in concept, in doctrine, not a technological development.

Technical advances, to be sure, appeared in the machine-gun during the period of World War I, but these were improvements and modifications rather than basic changes. The increased number of machine-guns in each British division represented an advance in doctrine carried out at tremendous cost in blood. Even when prompted by mounting casualties, revision of the conventional doctrine was not easy. As late as 1915 one British commander considered the machine-gun "a much over-rated weapon." Moreover, despite frequent German demonstrations of the machine-gun's value, he felt that two per battalion were "more than sufficient."[40] On the other hand, Brig Gen C. T. Baker-Carr, a British officer who played one of the leading roles in revising doctrine on machine-guns, probably recognized the real nature of the problem. He saw the delay in modifying military doctrine to fit the requirements of the new weapon as "the fault of the system" rather than "the fault of the individual." Baker-Carr possibly came even closer to the heart of the matter when he said, "The chief trouble at GHQ was that there was no one there who had time to listen to any new idea."[41] His observation is all the more revealing in that it echoes a sentiment expressed by Sir Percy Scott, "the Admiral Sims* of the Royal Navy." Admiral Scott considered the blindness of the Admiralty to new ideas a direct result of the failure of "administrative machinery" to provide "time to think of the needs of the future and how they should be met."[42] For want of "time to think" and for lack of an organization specifically charged with the function of relating doctrine to advances in weapons, the machine-gun, although a standard item of equipment in 1914, was not fully exploited until well into the middle of World War I.

The tank, like the machine-gun, came into prominence during World War I, but unlike the machine-gun it evolved almost

---

*William S. Sims, US commander of naval forces in Europe in World War I. He won the Pulitzer Prize in 1920 for his book *Victory at Sea* and was a leading advocate of innovation and reform in the Navy.

entirely within the war years. Interesting and pertinent though they may be, the details of the process by which the War Office (and the Admiralty, for that matter) were led to consider the idea of an armored tractor and develop it as a weapon lie somewhat beyond the horizon of this study. Nonetheless, the history of the tank, once it was produced in quantity and utilized in combat, closely parallels that of the machine-gun. It might well be argued that from the battle of the Somme in September 1916 until Cambrai in November 1917 the tank was in the stage of proof testing. But the reduction in casualties and the ground gained when tanks were used thereafter conclusively showed the new weapon to be a revolutionary contribution to warfare. It is true that at the end of 1917 the tank still had far to go, but it had reached a point where even as an imperfect and faulty mechanism it was capable of exerting a significant influence in battle. Even so, in April 1918, the Royal Tank Corps was reduced from 18 to 12 battalions because infantry reinforcements were falling short.[43] In the crisis British military leaders clung to accepted doctrine: they favored manpower over materiel in securing victory. And even after the crisis had passed and while there was "time to think," official opinion continued to favor traditional concepts. The Infantry was still considered "the arm which in the end wins battles," and the rifle and bayonet were thought to be the infantryman's "chief weapons."[44]

The same thought echoed officially in the United States, although the Surgeon General's statistics gave some evidence that the rifle and bayonet may not have been so important after all.[45] Military doctrine was slow to embrace the full implication of the tank. "I laugh at ideas," Marshal Foch is reputed to have said. "However good they may be, they possess value only insofar as they are translated into facts."[46] The tank was an idea; it had been translated into fact; yet its full value went unrecognized at the end of the war. Wars, it would appear, are governed not by the development of weapons but by such fractions of that development as have been recognized and incorporated into approved military doctrine.

The introduction of gas warfare presents a case somewhat similar to that of the tank. Two German scientists, Walther

Nernst of the University of Berlin and Fritz Haber of the Kaiser Wilhelm Physical Institute, worked out the details of production and application of poisonous gas for use in the field. Then on 22 April 1915, at a point somewhat north of Ypres where the French and British lines joined, the Germans released a gas attack along a five-mile front. The results were staggering. After a 15-minute attack some 15,000 troops were thrown into confusion, and a great breach opened in the Allied lines. The British and French forces managed to close the breach, but only after suffering 5,000 casualties and the loss of 60 field guns as well as other stores and equipment. In a war of position where every significant advance necessarily involved breaching the enemy's line as a preliminary condition, the gas attack at Ypres presented the German forces with an amazing opportunity. That they did not exploit the advantage resulted directly from a failure of the high command to adjust doctrine so as to meet the potential of the new weapon. But subsequent notable successes with gas—for example, the defeat of the British Fifth Army in March 1918—showed that the German high command was not always slow to learn from its own mistakes.[47] Statistics strengthen significantly the impression that the enemy in World War I recognized the full importance of relating doctrine with novel weapons. Figures compiled by the Surgeon General in the United States demonstrate that 27.3 percent of the casualties suffered by the AEF were from gas.[48]

In brief historical sketches, the pages above have shown that the pace at which weapons develop is determined by the effectiveness of the procedures established to translate ideas into weapons. The prior acceptance and application of the thesis that superior arms favor victory, while essential, are insufficient unless the "superior arms" are accompanied by a military doctrine of strategic or tactical application that provides for full exploitation of the innovation. But even doctrine is inadequate without an organization to administer the tasks involved in selecting, testing, and evaluating "inventions." The history of weapons in the United States is filled with evidence on this point.

For want of an adequate administrative organization in the Ordnance Department, as shown earlier, Federal troops in the Civil War fought with inferior weapons even though better arms were available. There were at least two major factors contributing to the ineffectiveness of the methods used by the Ordnance Department to select weapons. The first was the apparent inability of the successive authorities to establish either a sound organization or effective administrative procedures to accomplish the desired task. The second, the pressure of an obvious need for standardization in opposition to the continual pace of technological development, is typified by the comment of Secretary of War Joel R. Poinsett in 1838 when he declared that Ordnance should "suffer a paralysis" rather than be "exposed to frequent changes and fluctuations."[49]

The chief of ordnance was officially responsible for the "patterns, forms, and dimensions" of all items purchased by Ordnance, but it had become customary for the chief to rely upon a board of officers "to adjust the details." Until 1839 appointments to this board had been made from all the various arms of the service, but from that date on the Ordnance Board was composed exclusively of officers from the Ordnance Department.[50] While this decision undoubtedly improved the technical qualifications of the board's membership, it also deprived the board of the point of view of the branches that used its services. Although there were serious disadvantages in a board lacking the consumer's point of view, it might be argued that specialists, if working full time, could be expected to take a greater and more effective interest in improved weapons than any occasional and part-time board of constantly changing composition. Unfortunately, though, for the progress of weapons, as late as 1861 the chief of ordnance informed Secretary of War Simon Cameron that while the establishment of a permanent board was desirable it was impossible since all officers were engaged in the "pressing and indispensable duties of the Department." The chief of ordnance recommended that the plan to form a permanent board be "deferred to a future time."[51] It was decisions of this order that prevented federal troops from fighting with the best available weapons and resulted in an unissued surplus of 1,195,572 obsolete muzzle-loading muskets at the end of the war.[52] Here was quantity, not quality.

The organization and functioning of the Ordnance Board, critical as it may have been, were by no means the only aspects

71

of the administrative procedure that constituted the Ordnance Department's process for acquiring new weapons. Regardless of how well or how poorly any succession of ordnance boards may have performed their tasks, battle alone could be the final criterion of the value of a weapon, and this circumstance made necessary an adequate system for securing accurate reports from tactical units of the services in time of war and from military attachés and observers abroad during periods of peace at home. During the 10 or 20 years immediately preceding 1861, the Ordnance Department had sent occasional special observers to foreign nations to watch advances in weapons that then appeared in the United States only "tardily after being matured abroad." Nevertheless, as late as 1853, even while recognizing that the limited experience of this nation in actual warfare made the department necessarily dependent upon the military services of other countries for improvements in weapons, the chief of ordnance regarded the idea of sending a technical mission abroad as advantageous but unnecessary in view of the high state of perfection of the arms issued by the department.[53]

If the procedure for reporting on foreign experience with weapons and exploiting foreign technological advances was haphazard and ineffective, almost exactly the same could be said about the system that the Ordnance Department had for securing reports on the performance of weapons issued for use in combat. From the time of the Mexican War to 1861 there were few opportunities to secure operational reports. Thus little or nothing was done to establish a routing procedure for reporting back to the department the results of tactical experience with items in the field. In 1862 the chief of ordnance made an attempt to improve the situation. He asked his officers serving with troops in the field to keep daily notes of any "defects or deficiencies" in weapons and report them promptly with suggestions for "suitable remedies." This procedure, foreshadowing the system of rendering *Unsatisfactory Reports* that evolved many years later, had all the weaknesses of the latter system in that it depended entirely upon the initiative of officers in the field and revealed trouble only after it had happened.[54]

Probably the real beginning of scientific accumulation of data for ordnance came after the war, in 1867, when orders went out to all batteries of artillery requiring an exact and detailed report of each shot fired. Units were instructed to record the history of each gun, the weight of projectiles, and the quality of powder used, as well as other similar information, on blank forms provided for the purpose by the Ordnance Department."[55] A few years later an imaginative and resourceful chief of ordnance, Brig Gen Stephen Vincent Benét, demonstrated the real utility of a systematic collection of statistics as a basis for decisions regarding development of weapons. Using the figures compiled by the Surgeon General on casualties during the Civil War and reinforcing them with similar statistics from the Franco-Prussian War, General Benét argued that the saber and bayonet were no longer important weapons. Presentation of these facts started the movement that reduced the saber to the status of ceremonial gear.[56]

To pursue this line of thought further would be to write the history of the Ordnance Department. It is quite unnecessary to do so, for the essential elements in the problem of the development of weapons can be studied in detail from the period already mentioned. The experience of the department demonstrated the importance of establishing a concept of requirements—the military characteristics of a weapon—before beginning development. Similarly, experience had shown the importance of differentiating a good idea from the failure of that idea in a specific application. By the end of the Civil War there should have been no difficulty in recognizing the need for a service test to prove new weapons, for an adequate system to evaluate and report on performance in combat of new weapons, and for securing systematic reports on advances in foreign weapons. The problem of the organization and composition of an Ordnance Board, as well as the utility of statistical data on which such a board might base its decisions, could be studied in great detail before the turn of the century. In short, almost all of the problems that were to prove so vexing in the development of aerial weapons crowded the pages of Ordnance history.

The records of both the War and Navy departments were full of lessons of positive value to those responsible for the development of weapons in the years to come. Unfortunately, many of these lessons were buried in cluttered archives, virtually inaccessible to the officials who best could profit from them. Trained historians can sometimes bring the lessons to light but often too late to be of use. For example, James Phinney Baxter's analysis of the problem of developing weapons, which appeared in his naval classic, *The Introduction of the Ironclad Warship,* was not published until 1933, rather late to be of value to those charged with perfecting the aerial weapon. Nevertheless, it is perhaps significant that the substantial lessons to be garnered from the experience of the Ordnance Department were available, for the most part, in published form before the Wright brothers flew their first airplane. The evidence indicates that armies, war offices, and governments at the outbreak of World War I lacked effective systems for integrating the advances of science with the military machine. Anyone who seeks to evaluate the incorporation of the aerial weapon into the military establishment must recognize the problem as falling within this historical context.

Notes

1. This account is based upon Charles Oman, *A History of the Art of War in the Middle Ages,* vol. 1 (London: Methuen, 1898), 597–615.

2. Ibid., 400.

3. Ibid., 569.

4. Ibid., vol. 2, 67–124.

5. T. Wintringharn, *The Story of Weapons and Tactics from Troy to Stalingrad* (Boston: Houghton Mifflin, 1948), 29.

6. Brig Gen S. V. Benét, ed., *Annual Reports and Other Important Papers Relating to the Ordnance Department,* vol. 1 (Washington, D.C.: Government Printing Office [GPO], 1878), 381–82. Hereafter cited as *Ordnance Reports.* See also vol. 2, 1880, and vol. 3, 1890. The title varies for later volumes.

7. Ibid., vol.1, 435–36.

8. Ibid., vol. 2, 3–4.

9. Ibid., 8–9.

10. Ibid., 881.

11. Ibid., 669.

12. Secretary of War, *Annual Report,* 1860, Sen. Doc., 86th Cong., 2d sess., vol. 2.

13. *Ordnance Reports,* vol. 4, 842–45.

14. Ibid., 882–83.

15. Ibid., 893–94. See also F. A. Shannon, *The Organization and Administration of the Union Army: 1861–1865* (Cleveland: Arthur H. Clark, 1928), 142.

16. *Ordnance Reports,* vol. 4, 903.

17. Shannon, *Union Army,* 123, from *War of the Rebellion,* compilation of official records of Union and Confederate Armies (Washington, D.C., GPO, 1880–1901), ser. 3, vol. 5, 145.

18. B. H. Liddell Hart, *The British Way in Warfare* (London: Faber and Faber, 1932), 121–22 (hereafter *British Warfare*). See also E. P. Alexander, *Military Memoirs of a Confederate* (New York: Scribner's, 1908).

19. Shannon, *Union Army,* 108–9, 140. For pertinent comment on this problem in World War II, see J. P. Baxter III, *Scientists against Time* (Boston: Little, Brown, 1946), chap. 2.

20. Flavius Vegetius Renatus, *Military Institutions,* trans. John Clarke (London, 1767), bk. II, sec. xxv.

21. See, for example, Carl von Clausewitz, quoted in J. F. C. Fuller, *Armament and History* (New York: Scribner's, 1946), 1. See also J. F. C. Fuller, *The Foundations of the Science of War* (London: Hutchinson, 1926), 146 (hereafter *Foundations of War),* in which he quotes Thomas Carlyle's *Sartor Resartus,* "without tools he [man] is nothing, with tools he is all."

22. A survey of three representative military collections—the War Department Library, the National War College Library, and the Library of the American Military Institute—gives ample evidence of the comparative neglect of the problem by military writers until very recent years. Probably the most prolific but not necessarily the most influential of the few students of the importance of armament is Fuller.

23. Carl von Clausewitz, *On War,* trans. J. J. Graham from German 3d ed. (London, N. Trüber, 1873), vol. 2, bk. 2, 43, and vol. 3, bk. 5, 3.

24. Ibid., vol. 1, bk. 2, 130. See also Carl von Clausewitz, *Principles of War,* trans. H. W. Gatzke (Harrisburg, Pa.: Military Service Publishing, 1942), an attempt to distill "timeless principles," which is more pointedly futile for its failure to embrace the potentialities of the development of weapons.

25. Baron A. H. Jomini, *The Art of War,* trans. W. P. Craighill and G. H. Mendell (London, 1862). See also *Logistics* 1, no. 1 (October 1946).

26. Liddell Hart, 11, 93. See also F. Foch, *The Principles of War,* trans. J. de Morinni from 1903 French edition (New York: H. K. Fly, 1918). For an example of Foch's influence in favoring manpower over materiel, see Foch-Pershing cable of 23 June 1918, cited in J. J. Pershing, *My Experiences in the World War,* vol. 2 (New York: Frederick A. Stokes, 1931), 123.

27. Gen F. G. Herr, *L'Artillerie,* 4–6, quoted by Fuller in *Foundations of War,* 29.

28. G. Douhet, *The Command of the Air,* trans. Dino Ferrari from 1921 Italian ed. (New York: Coward McCann, 1942), bk. 1, chap. 1, 6.

29. Benedict Crowell, *America's Munitions; 1917–1918* (Washington, D.C.: GPO, 1919); and William Crozier, *Ordnance and the World War* (New York: Scribner's, 1920). Both of these authors spoke with semiofficial authority since they wrote from the records and experiences of the war in which each had important roles with regard to materiel.

30. Secretary of War, *Annual Report,* vol. 1, 1919, 28.

31. J. M. Scammell, "A History of the Army Industrial College" (master's thesis, Industrial College of the Armed Forces, 1947), passim.

32. The term *total war* is a generalization frequently abused. During World War II approximately 59 percent of industrial production in the United States (1942–44) was devoted to war purposes. See Department of Commerce, *Survey of Current Business* (February, 1946), 13. The belated formation in 1943 of the New Developments Division of the War Department General Staff, after considerable civilian pressure had been exerted, is but one example of the lack of military emphasis on superior weapons. Another sign of the comparative neglect of superior weapons may be seen in the curriculum of the Army Industrial College, which did not emphasize the critical importance of research and development until *after* World War II.

33. See, for example, Brig Gen E. McFarland, "Trend in Weapons Types and Design," *Journal of the Franklin Institute* 230, no. 4 (October 1940): 415.

34. Liddell Hart, 49.

35. Douhet, *Command of the Air,* bk. 1, 30. Liddell Hart, 121, has almost the same thought.

36. Fuller, *Foundations of War,* 23, 31.

37. *Ordnance Reports,* vol. 4, 190.

38. *Reports from British Field Officers Attached to the Japanese and Russian Forces in the Field,* vol. 2, 66, cited in Fuller, *Foundations of War,* 22. See also War Department General Staff, *Reports of Military Observers,* MID Report no. 8, pt. 6, March 1907.

39. J. F. C. Fuller, *The Reformation of War* (New York: E. P. Dutton, 1923), 86.

40. Brig Gen C. D. Baker-Carr, *From Chauffeur to Brigadier* (London: E. Benn, 1930), 87.

41. Ibid., 89.

42. Adm Sir Percy Scott, *Fifty Years in the Royal Navy* (New York: Geo. H. Doran, 1919), vi–vii. For a similar criticism of the administration of the War Office in Kitchener's time, see Graham Wallas, *The Art of Thought* (London: J. Cape, 1926), 137.

43. Fuller, *Reformation of War,* 116, and *Armament and History,* 140.

44. British Army Field Service Regulations, 1924, quoted by Fuller in *Foundations of War,* 30.

45. Report of Chief of Staff, *Annual Report of the War Department,* 1920, vol. 1. Gunshot and bayonet wounds show a comparatively low incidence in relation to casualties from other causes, e.g., gas.

46. Quoted by Maj Gen E. D. Swinton in *Eyewitness* (London: Hodder and Stoughton, 1932), 80.

47. Brig Gen A. H. Waitt, *Gas Warfare* (New York: Duell, Sloan, and Pearce, 1942), 21.

48. Fuller, *Armament and History,* 163; and *Reformation of War,* 110. See also Report of Surgeon General, *Annual Report of the War Department,* 1920, vol. 1.

49. *Ordnance Reports,* vol. 3, 366.

50. Ibid., vol. 3, 225.
51. Ibid., vol. 3, 226.
52. See above n. 17.
53. *Ordnance Reports,* vol. 2, 290, 397, 531.
54. Ibid., vol. 3, 438. The Unsatisfactory Report currently used in the USAF consists of an official form which units in the field are urged to use when reporting to higher headquarters on any unsatisfactory performance in equipment issued.
55. Ibid., vol. 5, 313.
56. Ibid., vol. 3, 101–2.

THIS PAGE INTENTIONALLY LEFT BLANK

Essay 6

Insights on Technology and Doctrine*

Let me begin with a fable for our times—a historical example of the interaction between technology and doctrine. Vannevar Bush, a pioneer in the computer revolution, who headed the US Office of Scientific Research and Development (OSRD) in World War II, has written pointedly of the "reactionary stubbornness" of military bureaucracies. As an example, he cites the English crusaders in the Holy Lands. There they encountered Saracens armed with composite bows of laminated bone and sinew. These Saracen bows, Bush observes, were "far better" than the English bows.[1] The English took samples of the Saracen weapons back home but then ignored them, continuing to use the yew wood longbow unchanged in any way for hundreds of years.

The obvious inference would seem to be that for want of a proper organization to assess a remarkable example of enemy technology, the medieval Englishmen lost an opportunity to secure a significant advantage over their enemies in Europe. This is a plausible inference, but it is quite erroneous. The Saracens' composite bow did indeed have a greater range, but its lighter arrows would not penetrate English armor. Moreover, the composite bow of bone and sinew was distinctly a dry climate weapon; if dampened, it became worthless, scarcely a weapon suited for service in most of Europe. The short composite bow was well adapted to the mobile warfare of the mounted Saracens with their hit-and-run tactics. The English yew wood longbow, on the other hand, was well adapted to the needs of the English infantry, the foot soldiers who almost invariably served in a defensive role.[2]

In short, each of these bows, as with all weapons, had its pros and cons—its advantages and disadvantages. What determined who won any given battle was not alone the advantages

---

*This essay was originally presented as a paper at a symposium in London sponsored by the Royal Air Force in June 1985 under the auspices of the RAF Historical Office.

79

conferred by the particular technology of the weapons in hand but the manner in which those weapons were employed. Which is to say, while technology is important, no less so is doctrine. The Saracens drove out the crusaders because they developed tactics that exploited the unique characteristics of their composite bows to best advantage, not because their weapons enjoyed an absolute superiority over those of the Christians.

As an aside I might observe in passing that the aura of success with the longbow that comes down from Crécy and Agincourt still appeals to our English friends. British commandos used the bow and arrow in Norway in World War II to eliminate isolated sentries silently. Bows were used again more recently in Africa to kill Mau Mau terrorists in the jungle.[3] But now back to my main point: technological advances in weaponry to be effective must be accompanied by appropriate doctrine. As we shall see, the relationship between the technology of weapons and doctrine is an interactive one that cuts both ways.

The essence of doctrine is that it springs from recorded past experience—the hard-won lessons of the past whether that experience is by one's own forces in actual combat, the recorded participation of foreign forces in combat, or experience derived from extensive peacetime maneuvers and exercises. But experience is elusive, hard to capture. There's an old epigram in my native New England which says, "experience is a wonderful thing; it helps us to recognize our mistakes when we repeat them." This may be just another way of voicing the philosopher George Santayana's comment that those who cannot remember the past are condemned to repeat it. By turning to some examples of the interrelationship between technology and doctrine in the field of airpower it should be possible to see how this has affected not only the procurement of hardware but also strategy and tactics.

We are all familiar with the revolution in aviation that took place in the middle 1930s. Rapid development in engines and airframes led to the appearance of bombers with speed and range that outstripped the fighters that had previously been deemed indispensable as escorts on the basis of experience in World War I. In the US Army Air Corps, the Martin twin-engine B-10 bomber and later the Boeing four-engine B-17 were examples of such aircraft. Without fighter escorts, it was obvious that these planes would have to carry self-sufficient defensive armament. Despite the prevailing Air Corps doctrine, which indicated that the majority of interceptor attacks on bombers could be expected to approach within a 30-degree cone aft of the tail, every US bomber deployed down to the outbreak of war in Europe made no provision for tail guns.[4]

This glaring contradiction between declared tactical doctrine and the aircraft actually produced is all the more surprising in light of the succession of Royal Air Force (RAF) bombers just then appearing with nose- and tail-gun installations. In the United States an alert congressman during an appropriations hearing as early as 1934 observed that the RAF already had some 200 aircraft with tail guns. To his dismay he learned that the Air Corps was not even thinking of conducting experiments on how to solve the problem of enemy attacks from the rear, admittedly the most probable angle of approach. Despite this congressional prodding, the Air Corps took no action. Not until the grim realities of World War II, as reported by the RAF, was the B-17 hurriedly modified to provide twin .50-calibre machine-guns in the tail.[5]

Many other prewar examples could be adduced, but this one should be sufficient to suggest that the US Army Air Corps lacked a suitable organization and effective procedures to formulate realistic doctrine and equate that doctrine to the design of aircraft. As a consequence, the aircraft procured by the United States were ill-suited to the demands of combat. With the coming of World War II, greater resources were available to the services—more money and more manpower—but the failure to appreciate the need for a well-honed organization to perfect doctrine still persisted. While one might have expected the harsh exigencies of war to have forced a greater recognition of the need for better ways and means of adjusting doctrine to changing technology, the problem continued to plague air arm authorities.

Canadian historian Brereton Greenhous has given us a splendid illustration of a typical disconnect between technological innovation and doctrine in his account of how the RAF—and the US Army Air Forces—reacted to the Luftwaffe

Stuka dive bomber.[6] Ironically, although the Luftwaffe had employed dive-bombers in World War I, it was the experience of Ernst Udet—who flew a Curtiss Hawk in the United States after witnessing a Navy dive-bombing demonstration—that subsequently persuaded Luftwaffe leader Hermann Göring to buy two Curtiss Hawks for testing. This in turn led to the publication of standard dive-bomber specifications in 1933, which eventuated in the Ju-87 or Stuka.[7] Although some skeptical officers pointed out that the Stuka would be vulnerable to ground fire during its prolonged dive and relatively easy prey to high-performance enemy fighters, Udet, who had become chief of the Luftwaffe Technical Office, put the Stuka into production, so it was available in large numbers for operations in Poland and in France.

Both British and US officials reacted strongly to the German use of dive-bombers in these two blitzkrieg campaigns. Apparently over impressed by newsreel pictures of Stukas screaming down on Allied tank formations, they rushed to place orders for dive-bombers rather than other more available types of aircraft. Soon the myth of the dive-bomber–tank combination was well established. As the anonymous author of *Diary of a Staff Officer* put it, "German dive bombers have proved irresistible."[8] A British tank commander rather soberly pointed out that it was Erwin Rommel's artillery, not the Stukas that gave him the most trouble. But there was no organization at hand equipped to undertake a thoroughly objective analysis of the evidence. So the myth sped on that Stukas could routinely knock out armor. By the middle of 1942, by which time the British authorities had finally become convinced that dive-bombing was a fizzle and nowhere near as effective as had previously been thought, the US Army Air Forces was proudly reporting that a large complement of dive-bombers had been deployed to the operating units!

While one might dismiss the bungled case of dive-bomber doctrine as an aberration—a panic reaction, no such excuse surely can apply to the commitment of US and British airmen to the whole concept of strategic bombardment—the central doctrinal stance of both services. Airpower zealots on both sides of the Atlantic left no doubt about this. As Air Commodore

L. E. O. Charleton put it in 1937, "air power is bombing capacity and nothing else," a statement he went on to bolster by adding that "an assessment of the air strength of a country should be based exclusively on . . . the number of its bombing squadrons."[9] Even for those of us willing to attribute a great deal of validity to the whole of strategic bombardment, it is not unreasonable to suggest that the realities of combat were to undercut substantially extreme views of this stripe.

But for all their enthusiasm for strategic bombardment, neither in the RAF nor the US Army Air Forces had the doctrinal implication of strategic bombardment been thought all the way through. To take but one example, neither of the two services had adequately recognized the crucially important role of aerial navigation and the technical means it required as an essential element in the business of getting bombs on designated targets.[10] As one RAF officer lamented in a letter to Cmdr Philip Van Horn Weems, the American guru of navigation, "the great trouble has been to obtain the active interest of senior officers in any matter connected with navigation."[11] After the war the senior commander of the US Army Air Forces, Gen Henry H. "Hap" Arnold, admitted that his units had entered the war "lacking any well-developed knowledge of . . . navigational techniques." Air Marshal Sir John Slessor, looking back when writing his memoirs after the war, was undoubtedly right when he suggested that the RAF stand on strategic bombardment prior to 1939 was largely "a matter of *faith.*"[12]

Faith in the efficacy of strategic bombardment may well have been justified, but the neglect of navigation as a vital aspect of the bombardment weapon system certainly underscores the absence of an organization and suitable procedures for subjecting the whole problem to the most rigorous analysis in all its ramifications. The officials involved could, of course, plead scarcity of funds. And we should sympathize with all who bore responsibility in the early months of the war when everyone was fairly overwhelmed by the exponential expansion that took place. But what about the mature organization that evolved as the war progressed?

How well did it cope with the problems of doctrine? One notable example comes from no less a body than the Joint Chiefs of Staff (JCS), the highest planning body for the armed forces of the United States. As late as October 1943, when the technology of the four-engine heavy bomber was highly advanced, the Far East War Plans Group prepared a paper on joint war planning for the Pacific area. This paper was reviewed and endorsed by the Joint War Plans Review Board for consideration by the joint chiefs.[13]

This document is worth quoting because it illustrates, rather shockingly, the lack of rigor which even at this late stage of the war seems to have plagued doctrinal thinking: "It has been clearly demonstrated in the war in Europe that strategic air forces are incapable of decisive action, and hence the war against Japan must rely upon victory through surface forces, supported appropriately by the air forces. Final victory must come through invasion of the Japanese home islands."[14] One can readily observe that this statement is presented in the form of an emphatic assertion, as if demonstrated as a matter of established fact, rather than as a matter of opinion or conjecture.

In reality, by October 1943, the potential of strategic bombardment had neither been proved nor disproved. The slow build-up of bomber strength and the long delay in securing escort fighters with sufficient range to accompany the bomber stream all the way meant that it was late in 1943 before truly massive and sustained attacks on the German heartland were at all feasible. The so-called "Big Week" all-out assault didn't come until February 1944.[15] How then is the bold assertion by the Far East Plans Group to be explained? By October 1943 scarcity of funds and lack of able manpower could no longer be used as excuses. Surely the JCS as the highest planning body in the armed forces by then had first call on the best brains in the services. Despite this, it is evident that the Far East paper reflected a lack of objectivity and intellectual discipline.

Fortunately, more dispassionate heads on the JSC rejected the defective reasoning of the Far East group and in December 1943, substituted a drastically revised statement as the official JCS position. This one declared: "Our studies have taken account of . . . the possibility that invasion of the principal Japanese islands may not be necessary . . . the defeat of Japan may be accomplished by sea and air blockade and intensive air bombardment from progressively advanced bases. The plan must, however, be capable of expansion to meet the contingency of invasion."[16]

The contrast between the two reports quoted here is instructive. Like the first quotation, the second one is a concept, a hypothesis. It deals in expectations, in possibilities. But the tone or treatment is entirely different. Where the initial Far East War Plans paper was dogmatic, an assertion, the revised JCS statement is conditional. It recognizes that the case for strategic bombing had not been demonstrated. Cautiously it left the door open to the possibility that invasion might be necessary if strategic bombing failed. What converts mere concepts into sound doctrine is evidence, sound evidence based on hard-won experience objectively interpreted. But have we formulated sound doctrine from that experience and made it the basis not only of our training but our actual practice in combat operations?

The combat experience of the US Air Force in Vietnam suggests otherwise. In the early days of US involvement there, the aircrews themselves plotted their routes to and from their targets. They varied their paths with each mission to keep the enemy guessing.[17] However, as the forces in Vietnam grew larger and the problems of coordination more complex, all such planning gravitated upward to higher headquarters. There, identical patterns of access and egress to and from the target were stipulated in the operational orders sent down to the squadrons *unchanged*, day after day. Not surprisingly, the loss rate went soaring upward. The headquarters planners even compounded the error by failing to change unit call signs for months on end, thereby giving the enemy a free gift of vital intelligence. To compound the error even further, they routinely scheduled strikes, day after day, for the same hours. This unchanging routine gave the enemy gunners complete freedom to program repair and cleaning sessions as well as periods for crew stand-down for times other than the totally predictable hours of attack. Whether these follies stemmed from laziness or ignorance on the part of the headquarters planning staff is unclear. But what is evident is that we are here dealing with a different kind of problem. Here it was not a question of formulating doctrine from operational experience but rather a matter of getting those in positions of authority to heed the doctrine that already filled the manuals with admonishments on the need for surprise, deceptions, and stratagems.

If it proves difficult to correlate doctrine with the available hardware when the threat of enemy action imposes a frightful urgency to the process, how much more difficult it is to derive doctrine in peacetime when the goal of an enemy is remote or lacking. Some years ago the US Air Force argued that the Army was encroaching upon its prerogatives, citing specifically operation by the Army of the valuable little cargo plane, the twin-engine C-7 Caribou, which could deliver loads to restricted areas with short and unpaved runways, and thus had proved to be immensely valuable to the Army.[18]

The Air Force protest was successful and all Caribou aircraft were transferred to Air Force control. Soon thereafter there appeared a spate of statistics, all showing that the Air Force had a much higher readiness rate for the Caribou, a much lower accident rate, and several other statistical indications that the Air Force could do a better job than the Army in operating the C-7. What did not appear in the statistics was the fact that the Air Force had doubled the manpower the Army had previously assigned to the job of maintaining this airplane. When interservice rivalry is involved, objectivity comes hard! And lack of objectivity is the death of sound doctrine.

Of course, service rivalry cuts two ways. About the time of the Caribou case, the US Air Force was experimenting with a project known as low-altitude parachute extraction system (LAPES)— using drag chutes to extract thousands of pounds of cargo from the rear of a C-130 Hercules transport.[19] At the same time, the Army was asking Congress for funds to procure substantial numbers of heavy cargo helicopters to perform the same kind of deliveries under Army auspices, under Army control. Surely we are not surprised to learn that the Army, which controlled the packing and rigging of the parachutes used in the LAPES experiment found ways to inject interminable delays in an effort to frustrate the whole experiment.

Intense interservice competition is healthy insofar as it stimulates improvements and novel solutions, but not if it prevents

us from obtaining objective evaluations of technological innovations. Other similar instances of doctrinal failures abound,
but the several presented above should be sufficient to set the
stage for an analysis of the factors that seem to underlie the
difficulty military forces have had in perfecting suitable doctrines to ensure the optimum exploitation of the weapons at
their disposal.

Broadly speaking, there are two essentials if military services
are to establish an effective system for relating technology and
doctrine. The first requisite, it would appear, is to ensure that all
responsible officers, not just those in positions of command but
their subordinates as well, must understand the nature of and
need for doctrine. The second requisite is to establish an organization with effective procedures for generating sound doctrine.
These prescriptions sound simple enough, but if the US Air
Force is at all representative in the years since World War II, despite intervening wars, we have never enjoyed much success in
our efforts. We still do not have a truly effective method for developing doctrine.

Putting the problems involved in the form of a series of
questions may spark discussion and stimulate a fruitful exchange of ideas:

1. How can we best ensure that responsible officers understand what doctrine is, why it is needed, and how it is derived? We issue manuals, but are they read? Are they
   cast in a form that makes them readable? Do our staff
   schools and war colleges communicate the doctrinal
   process effectively?[20]

2. How can we best ensure the development of sound procedures for *collecting* operational experience? Do we train
   officers to write objective after-action reports? Do the
   customs and practices of the service encourage genuine
   candor when this involves reporting mistakes, blunders,
   and errors?[21]

3. How can we best ensure that existing doctrine is revised,
   updated, when advancing technology modifies existing
   weapons? The Focke-Wulf 190 with its fuel injection system could go into an abrupt pushover and thus escape

87

from a Spitfire, which with its float carburetor, lost power in a similar maneuver. If Luftwaffe doctrine taught this evasion tactic for hard-pressed Focke-Wulf pilots, how long did it take for the German authorities to modify that doctrine when the P-47 with its Stromberg floatless carburetor appeared on the scene with no loss of power when going into negatives Gs with a sudden pushover?[22]

4. How best can we ensure that suitable doctrine is developed for radically new hardware, novel weapons, made possible by the application of hitherto unexploited technology? Here the path is strewn with obstacles. We design tests and conduct maneuvers to try out the new weapon; given our strong human propensity to lean on previous experience, how can we avoid designing a test that reflects our past experience rather than seeking the full potential of the innovation? When the results of our tests and maneuvers are recorded, how can we ensure that preconceptions and prejudice or partisan branch or service interests do not distort the substance of our reports? Can we be sure that institutional bias isn't coloring our findings?[23]

5. Can we encourage interservice and interbranch competition to stimulate imaginative innovation, yet at the same time ensure the candor and objectivity which are so essential in the analysis that leads to the formulation of sound doctrine?

These questions are by no means the sum total of problems associated with the complex relationship of technology and doctrine, but they should be sufficient to initiate some free-wheeling discussion on the problem.

Notes

1. Vannevar Bush, *Pieces of the Action* (New York: Morrow, 1970), 28.
2. Victor Hurley, *Arrows Against Steel* (New York: Mason/Charter, 1975), 135, 170, 201.
3. Ibid., 15.
4. I. B. Holley Jr., *Development of Aircraft Gun Turrets in the AAF, 1917–1944*, Historical Monograph B-69 (Maxwell AFB, Ala., 1945), 285–86.

5. House, *Hearings on War Department (Air Corps) Appropriations for Fiscal Year 1935,* 73d Cong., 2d sess., 14 February 1934 (Washington, D.C.: Government Printing Office [GPO], 1934), 535.

6. Brereton Greenhous, "Aircraft Against Armor. . . ." in Timothy Travers and Christon Archer, eds., *Men at War: Politics, Technology, and Innovation in the Twentieth Century* (Chicago: Precedent, 1982), 97ff.

7. Matthew Cooper, *The German Air Force, 1933–1945: An Anatomy of Failure* (New York: Jane's, 1981), 48–50. See also Adolf Galland, "Defeat of the Luftwaffe: Fundamental Causes," *Air University Quarterly Review* 6 (Spring 1953): 23–24.

8. Quoted in Cooper, 40.

9. Quoted in Williamson Murray, "British and German Air Doctrine Between the Wars," *Air University Review* 31 (March 1980): 57.

10. Monte Wright, *Most Probable Position: A History of Aerial Navigation to 1941* (Lawrence, Kans.: University Press of Kansas, 1972), 161–201.

11. Ibid., 200.

12. Sir John Cotesworth Slessor, *The Central Blue: An Autobiography* (New York: Praeger, 1957), 203–4.

13. Maj Gen Haywood S. Hansell, Jr., *The Strategic Air War Against Japan* (Maxwell AFB, Ala.: Airpower Research Institute, 1980), 18–19.

14. Ibid.

15. Frank Craven Wesley and James Lea Cate, *The Army Air Forces in World War II* (Chicago: University of Chicago Press, 1948–1958), 2: 308; 3: 30.

16. Hansell, 19.

17. Presentation by Col Peter Dunn, Air Force Historical Foundation, National Air and Space Museum, Washington, D.C., 12 April 1985.

18. Lt Col David Mets, interviewed by author, Maxwell AFB, Ala., 15 September 1982.

19. Ibid.

20. For some suggestive insights, see Gen L. Kuter, "The Education of Air Leaders," *Sperryscope* 13, no. 4 (1954): 6–9.

21. For insights on superior German practice in this area, see Williamson Murray, "The German Response to Victory in Poland," *Armed Forces and Society* 7 (Winter 1981): 289; and *Naval War College Review* 38 (January 1985): 74.

22. Robert Schlaifer, *Development of Aircraft Engines* (Boston: Harvard University, Division of Research, Graduate School of Business Administration, 1950), 523, 543.

23. For insights on this problem, see Maj Gen O. A. Anderson, "Source of Historical Examples," *Airpower Historian* (April 1958): 88. For another view, see Col Huba Vass de Czege, "Toward a Science of War," *The Art of War Quarterly* 5 (June 1983): 12–25.

THIS PAGE INTENTIONALLY LEFT BLANK

Essay 7

Of Saber Charges, Escort Fighters, and Spacecraft: The Search for Doctrine*

An aphorism of Frederick the Great—"Good fortune is often more fatal than adversity"—offers a lesson for us to ponder. The teachings of failure, which subvert old ideas and established facts, serve the military institutions of the future better than do successes. Failures teach humility and are the nurse of progress. Successes stimulate blind pride and complacent self-confidence, which invite failure in future battles. So let us turn to some historical failures and learn from them.[1]

To begin with, suppose we look to our horses. By the end of the Napoleonic era, there were four rather clearly defined functions of cavalry: the *charge,* galloping knee to knee, boot to boot, with lance or saber in shock actions akin to modern armor; *reconnaissance,* where horsemen served as the eyes of the army, probing out ahead of the main force to locate the enemy; *screening,* where small elements of rapidly moving horsemen could cover exposed flanks and serve as a trip wire against surprise moves by the enemy; and *strategic cavalry,* where large forces of horsemen deliberately avoided the enemy's main forces and penetrated deeply into the rear areas to disrupt communications, burn bridges, and destroy supply dumps and production centers while at the same time dislocating enemy plans and calculations.

All of these cavalry missions depended on two critical factors. First was the relative speed differential between a mounted horseman and the foot soldier, roughly three to one. Second, the success of cavalry was in varying degrees dependent on the inferior qualities of the muzzle-loading musket with its slow fire and short range. Unfortunately for the horsemen, scarcely a decade after Waterloo, the development of the conoidal

---

*This essay, reprinted from *Air University Review* 34 (September 1984), was originally presented as the opening paper at the first Annual Military Space Symposium held at the Air Force Academy in April 1981.

bullet (better known as the minié ball) drastically altered the military equation.[2] Rifled weapons with ranges of up to a thousand yards strongly suggested, at least to the observant, that the day of the cavalry charge was over. Even before the Civil War in the United States, some regular cavalrymen urged the elimination of the saber. Sabers, one wrote, are "simply a nuisance; they jingle abominably, and are of no earthly use." The Surgeon General's Civil War wound statistics certainly confirmed this view. After months of operations in which the Union forces suffered tens of thousands of bullet wounds, only 18 authenticated cases of sword injury could be identified.[3]

Probably the most successful cavalry action of the Civil War was a strategic raid by Gen James Wilson, who incidentally, became a major general at the age of 27. Leading a force of 14,000 cavalrymen armed with Spencer repeating rifles, Wilson set out from Tennessee. He cut a swath clear across Alabama tearing up rail lines and destroying arsenals, foundries, and supply dumps. On the few occasions when this fast-moving force was unable to evade Confederate concentrations, it fought dismounted.[4]

One would think that the experience of the Civil War in the United States would have drastically altered the conception of cavalry throughout the Western world. But the social prestige of crack cavalry regiments and their brave showing on parade made it difficult to read the historical record realistically. European military writers—one cannot say military *thinkers*—were inclined to blame poor leadership rather than faulty doctrine for the failures of cavalry in the face of rapid-fire infantry weapons.[5]

In Britain, toward the end of the nineteenth century, Lord Roberts*—the beloved commander in chief who was popularly known as "Sir Bobs"—saw the facts with a clear eye and directed the cavalry to abolish the lance and be prepared generally to act dismounted. But horsemen in a foxhunting country were not so easily dislodged.[6] The *Cavalry Journal* had been founded in 1904 in Britain for the express purpose of defending the notion that, even under modern conditions with rapid-fire weapons, cavalry was still extremely important in war. One

---

*Field Marshal Frederick Sleigh Roberts

observer, reviewing the first issue summed up the whole tone and temper of the enterprise succinctly:

> It is evident from the number of articles devoted to . . . the subject that the editors have deliberately elected to commence with an exposure of the ridiculous contention of the mistaken school of thought by whom it is fatuously asserted that the days of the Cavalry . . . are over; and at the same time to illuminate, if possible, the dense intellects of others who have merely failed to comprehend the true functions of cavalry in modern war.[7]

The strength of the cavalry lobby in Britain is evident when one notes that despite the commander in chief's directive, the 1907 *Cavalry Manual* continued to espouse the traditional doctrine: "The essence of the cavalry spirit lies in holding the balance correctly between firepower and shock action. It must be accepted in principle that the rifle, effective as it is, cannot replace the effect produced by the speed of the horse, the magnetism of the charge, and the terror of cold steel."[8] This romantic eyewash appeared in the official British Army cavalry doctrinal manual. Instead of providing a whetstone for contradictory opinion, the *Cavalry Journal* only reinforced the romanticism, asserting grandiloquently, in 1909, "the charge will always remain . . . it will be the cavalryman's pride to die sword in hand."[9]

Again, one would think that the experience of World War I would have spelled the virtual demise of cavalry. To be sure, horsemen did prove useful in certain peripheral theaters: Edmund Allenby in Palestine and the czarists in those vast areas of Russia where the nature of the terrain precluded vehicular traffic. But in the main theater on the Western Front, British cavalry divisions ate tons of costly fodder waiting for the day that never came when they hoped to exploit a breakthrough; 10,000 horses consume as much weight in fodder as the food for 60,000 infantrymen, so the logistical cost was high. None of this experience seems to have made much impression.

The Superior Board of the General Headquarters (GHQ), American Expeditionary Force, assembled after the Armistice to cull out the important doctrinal lessons of the war, concluded that there were few reasons to change the prevailing cavalry doctrine.[10] True, some advances had been made. US Army cavalrymen had substituted the Colt .45 for the saber.

As one wag somewhat sardonically commented, this was a case of mounting "the inaccurate on the unstable."[11] The same spirit prevailed in Britain. "What," fumed one irate cavalry officer, "replace the horse with a tank? Why you might as well attempt to replace our railway system by lines of airships!"[12]

But J. F. C. Fuller, the military historian and close student of doctrine, was more perceptive. The cavalry is doomed, he said, and must give way to the tank. With his broad knowledge of history, however, he foresaw difficulties in replacing the horse with armored forces. "To establish a new invention," he cautioned, "is like establishing a new religion—it usually demands the conversion or destruction of an entire priesthood."[13]

In the United States, the cavalry priesthood proved remarkably persistent. As late as 1938 Gen Walter Krueger, the chief of the US Army War Plans Division, was still opposing the formation of a mechanized cavalry division. The chief of cavalry, Maj Gen J. K. Herr, was more broad-minded. He favored the creation of mechanized cavalry provided this were not done by converting existing horse units. It was this kind of thinking that led to the presence of two regular horse cavalry divisions at the Army maneuvers in Louisiana in 1940—long after courageous but futile Polish cavalry lancers had been decimated when charging invading Nazi panzer columns.[14]

What can we learn from this cavalry story? By virtue of hindsight we can perceive many of the horsemen's failures with considerable clarity. Clearly, cavalry doctrine was not kept abreast of technological advance. Armies of the time lacked appropriate organizations and procedures to perfect suitable doctrines. Too often those who thought about the problem at all were swayed by romantic or emotional considerations and failed to assess the problem objectively.

Surely a rational, scientific approach would suggest the desirability and the necessity of a patient and exhaustive search for data from operational experience, at home and abroad—experience in wartime and in peacetime maneuvers. Logically, this data-gathering should be followed by a careful assessment of the evidence to screen out opinion and ensure a high degree of objectivity in the evidence from which one attempts to formulate doctrine.

What is doctrine? Simply this: doctrine is officially approved prescriptions of the best way to do a job. Doctrine is, or should be, the product of experience. Doctrine is what experience has shown usually works best.

Doctrine is not the same thing as dogma. Where dogma is frozen, fixed, unchanging, and arbitrary—based on authority, akin to "revealed truth"—doctrine is open-ended. Doctrine is subject to continual change as new developments, new experience, technological innovations, and the like, require us to reconsider and impel us toward a revised statement of official doctrine."[15]

In the abstract, it is not very difficult to describe what is needed to decide how best to apply the horse, the airplane, the spacecraft, or any other asset as a military weapon. We simply proceed in a truly scientific spirit in search of objective evidence on which to build our decisions. Unfortunately, what seems simple and straightforward when described in so many words turns out to be exceedingly difficult in practice.

To begin with, actual battle experience is elusive; oftentimes it turns out that even the participants are not sure what happened. It is difficult to be objective, to rise above the din, to attain true perspective. Further, by no means do all who participate record their experiences. Even those who do, may record them incompletely or inaccurately. Consequently, the so-called evidence that becomes available for analysis is all too often partial, fragmentary; and not infrequently a vital portion of evidence is missing. One of the drawbacks of history is that we cannot rerun the episode or the battle in the same way we can rerun a scientific experiment in the laboratory to pick up the observation we missed the first time around. In the long intervals between wars, we must rely on tests, exercises, simulations, and maneuvers—bloodless battles that only imperfectly provide the kind of evidence we need. As if these inherent drawbacks were not enough, other obstacles in our path make the search for objective data difficult and sometimes seemingly impossible.

Military organizations are not ideal instruments for use in the search for truth. Military organizations are hierarchical: two stars outrank two bars. But what does this really mean? Where matters of opinion are concerned, rank certainly has its privileges. Greater rank presumes greater experience and therefore greater respect for its opinions. Let us never forget, however, that this applies only to opinion. As Secretary of Defense James R. Schlesinger used to say, "you're entitled to your opinion but not to your own exclusive set of facts." Where we are dealing with questions of *fact,* two stars do *not* outrank two bars. Sometimes stars forget that bit of truth. One is reminded of that perceptive nineteenth-century soldier Gen Sir Edward Hamley, who cynically defined tactics as "the opinion of the senior officer present."[16]

Caricatured in this fashion, we all instantly recognize the absurdity of all attempts to impose the authority of rank on what are or should be matters of objective fact. Yet, absurd or not, the record of how technological innovations have been integrated into the armed forces as weapons is strewn with examples of wishful thinking and failures to distinguish fact from opinion. Our past is littered with examples of failures in mustering objective evidence for orderly, systematic, and dispassionate evaluation.

And why has this been so? Largely, it appears, because military men have been slow to devise organizations and procedures explicitly directed to the perfection of doctrine. Traditionally, armed forces have attracted activists, men generally better at "doing" than "reflecting." This is understandable; philosophers do not make good shock troops. What is more, philosophers and military intellectuals tend to give Delphic responses. They tend to speak ambiguously. They do not give clear-cut answers or easy-to-follow lessons learned; they speak only of insights. Military historians are exasperating fellows; they profess to help the decision maker, the activist military commander, to see more deeply into his problem. They are exasperating because, instead of simplifying the commander's problem, they only show him how much more difficult it is than it appeared at first.

To illustrate the trouble commanders have with intellectuals, I must digress a moment to recall Napoleon's dilemma in Russia. He had led the Grand Army deep into the enemy country and occupied Moscow, the symbolic heart of the nation. Winter was threatening, but the emperor wanted to remain in Moscow as long as he could for the advantage it gave him when negotiating the peace proposals he hoped the Russians would offer him. On the other hand, Napoleon knew he must extricate his army from its dangerously extended position before the Russian winter closed in. So he turned to his chief scientist, Pierre Simon Laplace, and asked him to determine how long the French troops might safely linger in Moscow. On the available meteorological data from past seasons, Laplace calculated that there was a 100-to-1 probability that extreme cold would not set in before 25 November. Napoleon acted on this advice and stayed. On the sixth of November the thermometer dropped precipitately, winter swept in with more than usual severity, and the French Army was virtually destroyed.[17]

Napoleon was clearly on the right track when he employed a leading scientist on his staff. But in this pioneering effort at operational research, he learned the hard way that even when one tries to be objective in looking for evidence from past experience, the process is fraught with difficulties.

The airplane that the Wright brothers brought to the Army in 1903 was a rather flimsy contraption. After looking it over, Gen Ferdinand Foch, who later became the supreme commander of the Allied Forces in France, dismissed it out of hand by stating: "That's good sport, but for the Army it is of no value."[18] Foch was no bonehead; he was a thoughtful student of warfare whose volume of *Principles* was widely used in war colleges. His spurning of the airplane was, however, a classic example of throwing out the baby with the bathwater. To be sure, the Wright brothers' aircraft was just a flimsy box kite with only the slenderest margin of weight-lifting capacity. If military intellectuals such as Foch failed to perceive the latent powers of the airplane, it is easy to see why officials in the United States had some difficulty in soundly conceptualizing the potential of this innovation at a time when the Army was still a horse-drawn institution.

How should the airplane be exploited? A good case could be made for visualizing aircraft as the logical successor of the horse. The speed differential the airplane enjoyed over infantrymen would enable it to perform many traditional cavalry missions to great advantage. The ability to fly over obstacles and avoid enemy blocking forces on the ground held high promise of performing the deep penetration, independent strategic mission into the enemy's heartland, a mission already well defined doctrinally by the cavalry. But the horsemen would have none of it. Already threatened by the appearance of the gasoline-powered truck and the scout car, the cavalrymen saw the airplane as just another challenge to their traditional perquisites. What is more, the noise and smell of internal combustion engines frightened their horses!

So the airplane was adopted by the US Army Signal Corps. There was a good deal of logic in this decision. In 1903, signalmen were the most scientifically inclined officers in the Army. Moreover, the decidedly limited lifting capacity of existing aircraft precluded any immediate application of airplanes to strategic missions requiring heavy bomb loads capable of significant destruction in the enemy's rear areas. It followed naturally, then, that the Signal Corps would develop the airplane to provide yet another tool, along with the telephone and telegraph, in the service of information.

Although it may have seemed logical at the time, the decision to assign the airplane to the Signal Corps was to have profound consequences. The Signal Corps was a service, not a combat arm. Its officers saw themselves as ancillaries, assisting the three combat arms to carry out their tactical missions. In this context it was virtually inevitable that the airplane would be developed as an observation platform. Airplanes would be employed as the eyes of the Army rather than as offensive weapons geared to a strategic mission in emulation of the strategic role already well defined by traditional cavalry doctrine.

At least in part as a consequence of this accident of organizational or institutional sponsorship, the Army emerged from World War I with a genuine appreciation of the importance of the airplane as a useful adjunct to the ground forces. On the other hand, the case for the airplane as a weapon of strategic potential had not been adequately demonstrated to the satisfaction of those in command.

The story of how a small band of zealots, true believers in strategic airpower, struggled for the next 25 years or more to implement their ideas is too well known to require repeating. Gen William "Billy" Mitchell as prophet and idol and his younger disciples, Henry H. "Hap" Arnold, William Andrews, Carl Spaatz, and Ira C. Eaker—all contributed to the struggle in varying ways. They deserve their place in history. However, the emphasis here is not to celebrate success but instead to look behind the facade of success to analyze failures. The purpose here is to understand better how doctrine may be kept abreast of technological innovation and examine how the Air Corps developed doctrine for strategic airpower.

The task of formulating doctrine fell largely to the faculty of the old Air Corps Tactical School. In many respects the problem confronting these men was not unlike the problem confronting those who are trying to devise suitable doctrine for space. With no more than an exceedingly slender base of actual combat experience with strategic bombardment in World War I, air arm officers had to extrapolate, making imaginative projections as to what bomber operations in the future would involve. The air arm officers were further handicapped by the usual and inevitable peacetime shortage of funds, which slowed the development of progressively better hardware.

Adversity, lack of funds, and limited numbers of men and aircraft put a premium on perfecting procedures to ensure that all experience was properly squeezed to produce its quota of information for use in concocting doctrine. Unfortunately, Air Corps officers too often seem to have been unaware of, or insensitive to, the need for developing rigorous standards of objectivity when assessing the meager shreds of available evidence. A brief look at a crucial episode at the Air Corps Tactical School will illustrate my point.

In the early years of the Tactical School when the memory of World War I was still fresh in everyone's mind, the boys in the Bomber Branch displayed considerable realism in their thinking. When they projected long-range strategic bombardment missions, they visualized fighter escorts going along to fend off enemy attacks. This view persisted at least down to 1930, but thereafter the picture changed radically. The bomber enthusiasts began to move into positions of power and influence in the Air Corps, and they secured additional funds for the development of significantly superior bombers.

The appearance of the Martin B-10 bomber, which could out-fly the older fighters in the Air Corps inventory, ushered in a whole new attitude. If the bombers could outrun fighters, what could stop them? Fired with a new enthusiasm, some of the bomber boys began to suggest that there was no longer a need to invest funds in other types of aircraft. By 1934 the official Air Corps text on "Air Force" was asserting unequivocally that the bomber was the principal weapon, and its offensive role was the principal mission of the air arm. The Air Corps text asserted that all other forms of aircraft could be developed only by diverting funds that otherwise could be used to perfect the bomber. Not surprisingly, the pace of fighter development lagged.[19]

Gradually it became an article of faith with the enthusiasts that the bomber was invulnerable. "A determined attack, once launched," said a Tactical School instructor, "is most difficult if not impossible to stop." An official umpire after an elaborate air defense exercise at Wright Field declared, "it is impossible for fighters to intercept bombers."[20] On the West Coast in 1933, Hap Arnold decided to put the issue to a test, pitting P-26 pursuits against B-12 bombers, improved versions of the Martin B-10. On the basis of this trial, Colonel Arnold concluded that pursuit aircraft would rarely intercept bombers and then only accidentally. He envisioned pursuit aircraft in the future as limited to operations against other pursuit or observation planes. "It is doubtful," he concluded, "whether such operations justify their existence."[21] This virtual dismissal of fighter aircraft was the conclusion of the man who would subsequently command the mighty Army Air Forces in World War II.

Not everyone was willing to swallow the results of Colonel Arnold's test so readily. At the Tactical School, the head of the Pursuit Branch was Capt Claire Chennault. He subjected Arnold's report to a thoroughgoing, objective analysis and observed that Arnold had stacked the deck, using an obsolescent fighter against the very latest model bomber. "Technical progress," Chennault observed, "within a very short time may make the estimates of time and place wholly obsolete. The principles involved, however, will remain constant." Then he proceeded to enumerate the factors that should enter into a determination of the ability of pursuit aircraft to intercept bombers: the type of airplanes on hand, the location of their airfields, the availability of a warning net to give timely information on the location of the attackers, weather conditions, and the relative firepower of the opposing forces.[22]

Chennault concluded, on the strength of his analysis, that what the Air Corps needed was a single-place fighter with substantially extended range. This would facilitate interception of attacking bombers and at the same time would permit fighters to serve as escorts for bombers on long-range strategic missions into enemy territory. Subsequent events were to confirm the validity of Chennault's objective analysis. Unfortunately, Col Oscar Westover, the commander of the General Headquarters Air Force, the strategic air arm of that day, chose to ignore Captain Chennault's findings while accepting Colonel Arnold's highly subjective conclusions, which rested more on opinion than fact. Bombers, Westover asserted in his official report, can accomplish their mission "without support."[23]

The failure of those in command in the Air Corps to insist on the most rigorous analysis of the available evidence when developing bomber doctrine was to have the gravest consequences when World War II broke out. Bomber doctrine, when subjected to the brutal test of actual warfare, was found wanting. The Royal Air Force (RAF), while attempting daylight bombardment missions beyond the range of fighter escorts, suffered prohibitive losses. So appalling were these losses that the British authorities switched their doctrine and limited their deep penetrations to night raids when interception was infinitely more difficult. The survival rate went up at least temporarily, but there was a sharp decline in their ability to find and hit strategically significant targets; this decline went far to nullify the concept of strategic airpower.

These facts were known to the Americans well before Pearl Harbor, but the knowledge did not bring about an alteration of the prevailing bomber doctrine. When Gen Carl Spaatz took the first elements of the Eighth Air Force to England in the summer of 1942, he faced a painful dilemma. On the one hand, RAF leaders with combat experience behind them asserted that daylight bombing could not be done without unacceptable loss. On the other hand, Air Force doctrine, as yet

101

untested and resting largely on faith, held that daylight precision bombing would be successful. The bombers would get through to perform their strategic mission without escorting fighters if that mission required penetrations beyond fighter range. Which view was the right one? Only a test would decide.

So the Eighth Air Force began its tentative probing of Hitler's Fortress Europa with the limited resources at its disposal. The first few missions were successful. Not until the tenth mission did the bombers suffer a loss. These were shallow penetrations close to the coast and within the range of escorts. In October 1942, a 38-bomber raid struck German targets in France accompanied by 400 escorting fighters. Not surprisingly, the raid was a success. But what did such raids prove? Did they warrant the optimistic report sent back to the United States that "day bombers in strong formation can he employed effectively and successfully *without fighter escort*"?[24]

After a mere 14 heavily escorted shallow penetrations, the commander of the Eighth Air Force made an inferential leap, reaching the unwarranted conclusion that bombers could successfully perform strategic missions without fighter escorts. Clearly, this faulty inference was an act of faith, not logic, but the dreadful consequences were to be masked for several months by a number of circumstances. Throughout 1942 and during the early months of 1943, three-quarters of the German fighter force was tied up in Russia or North Africa. Moreover, diversions of cadres to build up Allied air units in North Africa weakened the Eighth Air Force so seriously that it was unable to mount a large-scale assault for many months. As late as February 1943, an average of only 70 bombers was available for each Eighth Air Force attack on the Continent. So a true test of bomber doctrine was deferred.[25]

The Germans, meanwhile, were developing some formidable defenses. They improved their radar screen, arranged for a more appropriate positioning of fighter bases, and perfected the lethal tactic of nose attacks on incoming bombers whose frontal firepower was then deficient. These actions on the part of the Germans began to take their toll.

During the summer of 1943, loss rates for Eighth Air Force bombers soared sickeningly. The Schweinfurt raid suffered

28.2 percent losses with 50 percent of the survivors requiring extensive repairs, which delayed launching of further attacks. Statistical studies quickly showed that unescorted raiders suffered losses seven times greater than those undertaken with escorts.[26] That the Eighth Air Force continued to press its strategic assault in the face of these devastating losses is a tribute to the courage of the crews if not exactly a monument to the existing system for devising appropriate doctrine.[27]

As we know, the solution to the escort problem was the drop tank. The P-47 had an initial range of only 175 miles. By expanding internal tankage, this range was extended to 230 miles. During July 1943, by adding 75-gallon drop tanks, the maximum range was extended to 340 miles. By February 1944, hanging on two 150-gallon drop tanks gave the P-47 a range of 475 miles. By then, the P-51 with drop tanks was going 560 miles—all the way to Berlin.[28]

If the drop tank was such an obvious solution to the problem of providing long-range escorts, why was it so long in coming? Wasn't it obvious at the time? Technically, there were many problems to solve. Someone had to design sturdy pylons and bracing to prevent buffeting by the tank in flight and to devise a valve to control the internal static pressure of the tanks. Another problem was that of installing pumps, which proved necessary when extracting fuel above 20,000 feet. One model drop tank involved 159 parts, including its mounts and external plumbing. This required the services of 43 different manufacturing firms.[29] These, of course, were all perfectly normal developmental problems. Given time, each of the difficulties could be surmounted.

More serious, however, was the conceptual failure that lay behind the decision to use drop tanks. In February 1939, when a manufacturer came in with a scheme for developing drop tanks, the chief of the Air Corps, Hap Arnold, decreed that "no tactical airplane will be equipped with droppable auxiliary fuel tanks." More curious still is the decision of the chief of the Plans Division in the Office of Chief of the Air Corps, who in March of 1941 turned down a proposal to add drop tanks to extend the range of fighters. By this date the RAF had already abandoned daylight bombing in principle, and the challenge to existing Air Corps doctrine was evident.[30]

The officer who made this fateful decision in 1941 was none other than Carl Spaatz. The document that articulated his disapproval spelled out his reasoning. "It is believed that," he wrote, "to permit carrying bombs or drop tanks would make for unnecessary weight and operational complexities incompatible with the mission of pursuit." The document further noted that the accretion of "extraneous details" not only would give aircraft designers "confused ideas" regarding the essential requirements for fighter aircraft but would also provide opportunities for "improper tactical use" of these airplanes.[31]

Literally hundreds of crewmen lost their lives because escort fighters of suitable range were not ready when needed. The lack of escort fighters jeopardized the whole effort to prove the feasibility of strategic airpower. What an irony that he who was to command the Eighth Air Force and suffer the brutal losses incurred in ramming home the Combined Bomber Offensive in 1943 and 1944 had it in his power in 1941 to provide the solution but did not.

I wondered who had done the staff work that lay behind this document signed by Spaatz. The working papers in the archives gave the answer—the initials were those of Hoyt S. Vandenberg, who would later become the second chief of staff of the newly formed postwar Air Force, following on the heels of General Spaatz. Vandenberg, before coming to the Plans Staff, had been an instructor in the Pursuit Branch at the Air Corps Tactical School. Manifestly he had not inherited Captain Chennault's gift for rigorous and objective analysis.

The story of how doctrine was devised for the airplane bears a painfully striking resemblance to the story of how doctrine was or was not developed for the horse cavalry. I conclude this foray into history by attempting to distill a few useful insights from the record of experience and hope that even a past on horseback may have a message of significance today.

We are on the verge of a great age in space when it will be of the utmost importance to exploit the spacecraft as a weapon to its fullest potential in our struggle for survival. On the analogy of the horse and the airplane, we must explore the full range of the offensive and defensive capabilities of spacecraft and study no less avidly their limitations. Again, on the analogy of the airplane, we must not delay our effort to conceptualize the eventual combatant role of spacecraft even if current treaty obligations defer the actual development of hardware.

If the record of the past tells us anything, it is almost certain that we shall make as many mistakes in formulating space doctrine as we did with cavalry doctrine and airpower doctrine if we do not first get our house in order. We must ensure that we build a truly effective organization for formulating doctrine and that it is staffed with the best possible personnel.

What is a sound organization? Ultimately, no organization is better than the procedures devised to make it function.[32] Yet, on every hand in the armed forces today, we see men in authority assigning missions and appointing leaders to fill boxes on the wiring diagram while seriously scanting the always vital matter of internal procedures. It is the traditional role of command to tell subordinates *what* to do but *not how* to do it; nonetheless, it is still the obligation of those in authority to ensure that the internal procedure devised by their subordinates meets the test of adequacy.

And what do we mean by the best people? We must have officers who habitually and routinely insist on objectivity in their own thinking and in that of their subordinates. This does not rule out imagination and speculation by any means. But we must have officers who insist on hard evidence based on experience or experiment in support of every inference they draw and every conclusion they reach.

We need officers who will go out of their way to seek and welcome evidence that seems to confute or contradict the received wisdom of their own most cherished beliefs. In short, we need officers who understand that the brash and barely respectful subordinate who is forever making waves by challenging the prevailing posture may prove to be the most valuable man in the organization—if he is listened to and providing his imagination and creativity can be disciplined by the mandate that he present his views dispassionately and objectively.

As wise old Gen Sir John Burnett-Stuart put it to B. H. Liddell Hart shortly after being given command of the British experimental armored force in 1926: "It's no use just handing over to an ordinary Division commander like myself. You must [assign] . . . as many experts and visionaries as you can; it doesn't matter how wild their views are if only they have a touch of the divine fire. I will supply the common sense of advanced middle age."[33]

Notes

1. Jay Luvaas, *The Education of an Army* (Chicago: University of Chicago Press, 1964), 3. See also Maj Gen W. B. Hazen, *The School and the Army in Germany and France* (New York: Harper and Brothers, 1872), 189.

2. *Encyclopaedia Britannica*, 1946 ed., 70ff.

3. J. T. Hubell, ed., *Battles Lost and Won: Essays from the Civil War History* (Westport, Conn.: Greenwood Press, 1975), 107, 139.

4. J. K. Herr and Edmond S. Wallace, *The Story of the US Calvary, 1775–1942* (Boston: Bonanza Books, 1953), 138–40; and Jay Luvaas, *The Military Legacy of the Civil War* (Chicago: University of Chicago Press, 1959), 37–44.

5. Dennis E. Showalter, "Prussian Cavalry, 1806–1871: The Search for Roles," *Militärgeschichte Mitteilungen* 19 (1976): 14.

6. Luvaas, *Education*, 316.

7. Ibid., 198–99.

8. Ibid., 316.

9. Quoted in John Ellis, *Cavalry: The History of Mounted Warfare* (New York: Putnam, 1978), 173.

10. George T. Hoffman, "Tactics vs Technology: The US Cavalry Experience," *Armor* 82 (September 1973): 11.

11. Edward L. Katzenbach, "The Horse Cavalry in the Twentieth Century: A Case Study in Policy Response," *Public Policy* 8 (1958): 127.

12. Luvaas, *Education*, 355.

13. Ibid.

14. Hoffman, 14; and Herr and Wallace, 256.

15. For a detailed discussion, see I. B. Holley Jr., "The Doctrinal Process," *Military Review* (April 1979), 2–13.

16. Luvaas, *Education*, 153.

17. Ibid., 45–46.

18. B. H. Liddell Hart, *Foch: The Man of Orleans* (London: Eyre and Spottiswoode, 1931), 47. For a parallel view by a US Army officer as late as 1911, see Aaron Norman, *The Great Air War* (New York: Macmillan, 1968), 21–22.

19. T. H. Greer, *The Development of Air Doctrine in the Army Air Arm, 1917–1944*, USAF Historical Study no. 89 (Maxwell Air Force Base, Ala.: Air University Research Studies Institute, 1955), 55.

20. Ibid., 55–56.

21. Lt Col H. H. Arnold to chief of air corps, Maj Gen Benjamin D. Foulois, 26 November 1934, Pursuit Aviation, 4686-33 A and B, Simpson Historical Research Center, Maxwell AFB, Ala. See especially paragraph 13. [NOTE: the Simpson Historical Research Center is now the Air Force Historical Research Agency (AFHRA).]

22. Capt Claire L. Chennault to commandant, Air Corps Tactical School, 7 March 1935, AFHRA 4686-35 A and B. See also Chennault's undated notes: Interceptors: Pursuit Aviation, AFRHA 4647-97, and his mimeographed text, "The Role of Defensive Pursuit," 1933, AFHRA 4773-10.

23. Greer, 59, 65. See also Robert F. Futrell, *Ideas, Concepts, Doctrine: A History of Basic Thinking in the United States Air Force, 1907–1964* (Maxwell AFB, Ala.: Aerospace Studies Institute, Air University, 1971), 35.

24. Wesley Frank Craven and James Lea Cate, *The Army Air Forces in World War II*, vol. 2, *Europe: Torch to Pointblank* (Chicago, University of Chicago Press: 1949), 219, 222.

25. Ibid., 233, 237, 308.

26. William Emerson, "Doctrine and Dogma: Operation Pointblank as Case History," *Army*, June 1963, 55–56.

27. Craven and Cate, 635. As late as May 1943, the US Army Air Forces Policy Group was still contemplating strategic attacks on Germany "usually unsupported by fighters because of their deficiency in range."

28. Spaatz Report, vol. 2, 1947, AFHRA 106-90, 2–4. These figures differ in some particulars with those found in Report of Lt Gen Ira Eaker, Eighth Air Force, 20 February 1942 to 31 December 1943, AFHRA 168, 61–63. See also Emerson, 60.

29. *History of Air Service Command, Eighth Air Force*, vol. 3, chap. 5, AFHRA 519.01, 1942–45, 60–63.

30. Air Technical Service Command (ATSC) case history, "Droppable Fuel Tanks: 1939–1943," summary narrative and document 11, chief of Air Corps TWC, 16 May 1939; document no. 20, Lockheed Report, 19 September 1941; and document 21, K. B. Wolfe, "Production Engineering Section, 9 December 1941," AFHRA 202.6-6. For subsequent developments, see ATSC case history, "Fighter Aircraft Range Extension Program," pts. I and II, AFHRA 202.2-11. See also Brig Gen H. S. Hansell Jr., oral history interview, 19 April 1967, AFHRA K239.0512-629, 22–26.

31. Chief, Plans Division to executive, 10 March 1941, AFHRA microfilm reel A1422, frame 1386-7.

32. For an extended discussion of the procedures involved in formulating doctrine, see I. B. Holley Jr., "The Doctrinal Process," *Military Review*, April 1979, 2–13.

33. B. H. Liddell Hart, *The Liddell Hart Memoirs*, vol. 1 (London: Casell, 1965), 112; *History of Air Service Command, Eighth Air Force*, vol. 3, chap. 5, AFHRA 519.01: 1942–45, 60–63.

THIS PAGE INTENTIONALLY LEFT BLANK

Essay 8

Looking Backward to See Ahead in Space: Reflections on the Need for Space Doctrine*

The text for this paper comes from the motto of the Air University: "We Advance Not Bound by Tradition." What were the founders of that institution thinking when they adopted this motto? Were they under the spell of the then but recently exploded atom bomb? Did they somehow conclude that nuclear weapons and airpower had made all previous history obsolete? If so, they had considerable sanction from a number of eminent students of war. Even so distinguished a philosopher of polemics as Maj Gen J. F. C. Fuller declared at the time that the revolutionary impact of the atom bomb had relegated all past military history "to the dustbin of obsolete things," as he expressed it, "there to join witchcraft, cannibalism, and other outgrown social institutions."[1] Any such sweeping and total dismissal of the whole of history is bound to catch the attention of a professional historian. But historians need not panic; fulminations of this sort really aren't new. Long before the advent of nuclear weapons, Giulio Douhet, in his well-known plea for airpower, *Command of the Air,* saw no utility in military history because, as he reckoned, the airplane made the whole of the past obsolete. "We have to follow an entirely new course," he wrote, "because the character of future wars is going to be entirely different."[2]

Whatever the founders of the Air University may have been thinking when they selected their motto, in the generation that has marched past since then the utility of a historical perspective has successfully reasserted itself. Douhet has been repudiated on many points as a faulty prophet. Our experience in World War II showed that many of his basic assumptions were fatally flawed. And, Fuller to the contrary, our war colleges continue to find inspiration and insight in the study

---

*This essay was presented as a paper at the Second Annual Military Space Symposium held at the Air Force Academy in October 1982.

of the past. Indeed, the Air Force, in the early 1980s, launched a major program, Project Warrior, to foster the study of history throughout the service at every echelon from sergeant to four-star general.

But this very enthusiasm for the historic past leads me to a note of caution. In the words of the old Scots preacher, "history makes good ballast but poor cargo." It is all too easy to go to the other extreme and find, in history, evidence (examples) that "prove" almost anything we wish to prove, to support almost any policy we wish to sanction. As Prince Hohenlohe,* the famous 19th century German artillerist pointed out long ago, "it is well known that military history, when superficially studied, will furnish arguments in support of any theory or opinion." Clausewitz himself warned us that the citation of historical examples provides only the *semblance of proof.*[3]

Let me illustrate this pitfall in history with some homespun examples. Proverbs, adages, and maxims are pithy sayings that purport to reflect folk wisdom, the congealed truths derived from long human experience—which is what we call history. Take, for instance, that adage right out of Ben Franklin's *Poor Richard's Almanac:* "Many hands make light work." We are quite willing to accept that obvious truism. But no sooner have we uttered it than we recall another adage: "Too many cooks spoil the broth." So too, when we confidently admonish: "Look before you leap," we are confounded when we recall that "he who hesitates is lost."

So we are forewarned. History is by no means obsolete; it is still capable of offering us important and highly useful perspectives, but we must be everlastingly cautious in using history, for it is seductively easy to misinterpret and misuse.

Now then, what in heaven's name has history to tell us about space? After all, the whole of the effective space effort falls well within the compass of living memory—within the life span of most of readers of this volume—even if we start counting with Robert Goddard's first crude efforts to attain, as he put it in his epoch-making Smithsonian paper, on reaching "extreme alti-

---

*Kraft Karl August Eduard Friedrich, Prinz zu Hohenlohe-Ingelfingen

tudes."[4] A backward glance at the evolution of aircraft as
weapons for national defense can bring us many insights that
can illuminate some of the central issues confronting our space
efforts today and tomorrow. To this end, it will be useful to go
back to the early days of aircraft, back to a period of infancy
comparable to the initial stages of our reach into space.

While doing research in the splendid library at the Air University, I stumbled, entirely serendipitously, upon a most interesting article. It was entitled "Aircraft and War" and appeared in the December 1913 issue of the *Infantry Journal.* It
was written by a young lieutenant—a West Point graduate
named Henry "Hap" Arnold—who would become the commanding general of the US Army Air Forces in World War II. In
his explication of aircraft and war Lieutenant Arnold had very
little solid historical experience to go on. The British, French,
and Germans had all experimented with "aeroplanes," as he
called them, in recent maneuvers. And there had been some
limited wartime use of aircraft in Tripoli and the Balkans. So
Lieutenant Arnold proceeded cautiously. Actual wartime use
confirmed the utility of aircraft for reconnaissance, he declared. Beyond that, however, he saw their use as "more or
less a matter of conjecture."[5] Then he went on to enumerate
the other roles for aircraft in their probable order of importance after reconnaissance. These included "warding off hostile aircraft," or what we would call air superiority. Then came
messenger service; observation and adjustment of artillery
fire; carrying supplies; and, finally, offensive operations. Note
in particular that he who would one day become one of the
high priests of bomber doctrine placed "offensive operations"
in the last and lowest priority.

The low expectations Lieutenant Arnold held for offensive
operations probably reflected the severely limited lifting capacity of the box-kite configurations of the then contemporary
airplanes. This is more or less evident in his further remarks:
"the actual damage that can be done to objects on the ground
from an airplane is very limited. But if 200 or 300 bombs are
dropped in or around a column of troops, there will be some
confusion and demoralization even if the damage is slight." We
are reminded of how many unknowns there still were in 1913

when Lieutenant Arnold goes on to say, "it is not thought that opposing aviators will try to ram each other in the air." We may smile at this today, but readers should recall that only a few years earlier highly placed naval officers were seriously debating the feasibility of arming cruisers with bow rams to disable enemy fleets.[6]

With 20/20 hindsight we smile condescendingly at Lieutenant Arnold's rather fuzzy vision of the on-rushing future. But then we stop and ask ourselves: In the infancy of the space age, is our vision of the future any clearer? On one point Lieutenant Arnold was lucidly clear. Despite the then current limitations of the box-kite aeroplane, despite its technical crudity in 1913, he saw and boldly asserted its claim to becoming the *fourth* combat arm—taking its place with the classic triad: the Infantry, the Cavalry, and the Artillery.

I hasten to add that not everyone in military circles accepted this or any other role for aircraft. Selfish or partisan branch preferences can blind even the most dedicated soldiers to the potential of novel weapons. Only a few years before, in 1909, the year the Army bought its first airplane, a farsighted infantryman, one Capt John A. Taylor, suggested in the pages of the *Infantry Journal* that aeroplanes might soon be able to perform the most important duty of cavalry—which he saw as "penetrating the fog of war to locate the heads of marching columns of the enemy."[7] This seemingly innocuous suggestion immediately sent the blood pressure of the cavalrymen soaring upward. The *Cavalry Journal* promptly published an editorial in outraged reply, protesting that Taylor's article didn't deserve serious consideration. How dare he tamper with the sacred functions of the horse cavalry?[8] The editors of the *Cavalry Journal* imperiously swept Taylor and his proposal to oblivion, boldly asserting that such an article should have been barred from the pages of a professional publication. The clear implication of the editorial was that the *Infantry Journal* had committed a serious breach of service propriety in printing Taylor's article in the first place.

From the perspective of the present we may find this rather blatant example of bigotry and narrow branch prejudice rather quaint—more amusing than harmful. But such historical instances prod us into thinking about similar situations closer to the present. Were the "battleship admirals" who resisted diverting funds from battleships to carriers in the between-war years any less narrow or any less guilty of branch partisanship? Capt Paul Schratz, a distinguished Navy submariner as well as a scholar, has pointed out that in the 36 months immediately prior to World War II, not one single article appeared in that excellent professional journal, the *Proceedings* of the US Naval Institute, which so much as suggested that the carrier might just possibly replace the battleship as the backbone of the fleet.[9] Or again, coming down in time to the years after World War II, do we find a parallel to those battleship admirals in "bomber generals"? Did bomber generals resist the development of the cruise missile because it was a competitor for funds that might otherwise go to bombers?[10]

These brief glimpses into history should make clear that it is folly to expect the record of the past to deliver us neat little packages called "lessons of history," tidy prescriptions or axioms that will tell us precisely what to do with some vexing problem tomorrow. Amongst historians it is a commonplace that one doesn't look to historical experience for answers. One turns there for questions—provocative questions that stimulate our thought and prod us into probing more deeply than we might otherwise be led to do.

All of us will probably agree that one of the most pressing problems confronting us as we escalate into the age of space is this: What organizational structure is best suited to the exploitation of space as an aspect of national defense? Should SAC [Strategic Air Command],* with its splendid track record of aggressiveness and exacting professionalism, have been the chosen instrument? Was a separate "Space Command" the best solution? Should such a command have taken over the research and acquisition functions for space from Systems Command,† given the unusual character of the hardware? If a separate command

---

*Elements of SAC have been absorbed in the US Strategic Command and the Air Combat Command.

†Now a part of the Air Force Materiel Command

is the approved solution, by the same logic, why not a separate "Space Force" entirely apart from the existing Air Force?

These are vexing questions. They insistently demand answers. As we grapple with them, surely we will be grateful for any insights the record of past experience may shed upon them. Insights, I say, *not* answers. We shall have got our money's worth from Project Warrior and other similar efforts if our reading of history goads us into asking the right questions.

By "right," I mean those searching questions that lead us to anticipate at least some of the false steps that continually lure us into seemingly easy solutions—which so often turn out to be, at the least, blind alleys, and, at the worst, downright disasters. Let me just propound a few questions raised by a cursory reflection on the history of the air arm.

When Lt Hap Arnold was groping tentatively into the unknown future of the aeroplane in 1913, the Army authorities already had decided to assign the aviation mission to the Signal Corps. What were the implications of taking that organizational turn in the road? The Signal Corps was *not* one of the combat arms; it was a *service*—one of the ancillary branches that render support to the combat arms. That decision, allocating aircraft to the Signal Corps, was to play a critical role in determining the future of the air arm for many years to come.

The organizational or institutional bias implicit in being a *service* seemed inexorably to warp the conception of the role aircraft were to play in the years ahead. As the principal agency for communication or the transfer of information, it was entirely natural for the Signal Corps to stress the support role of the airplane, the gathering of information—aerial photography, observation, reconnaissance. The airplane provided the eyes of the Army in a new and wonderfully enlarged way. Indeed, airplanes proved to be far better eyes, more versatile, faster, and with greater range, than any eyes the Army had ever had before.

Thus, it turned out that even after the informing experience with airpower in World War I, the chief of the Air Service, American Expeditionary Force (AEF), still regarded observation as the "most important role" of aircraft.[11] Nor was this empty verbiage; the record of aircraft acceptances by the Army in 1920 confirms the status: a total of 1,000 observation aircraft entered the inventory but only 112 pursuit and 20 bombers.[12]

There were a number of reasons why the Army gave primacy to observation and related close air support roles. One of the principal reasons lay in the fact that the Army lacked an adequate organization and method for the systematic analysis of its operational experience. It was, therefore, ill-equipped to develop a sound body of doctrine. Since the experience of the AEF with aviation, especially with strategic bombing, was exceedingly brief, deriving sound doctrine was a difficult task at best. So the chief of the Air Service simply mirrored the major body of experience, which was in observation, and failed to see the enormous potential hinted at in the limited body of experience with strategic bombing.

There was, of course, a very good reason for assigning aircraft to the Signal Corps. In 1909 that service was one of the most progressive, one of the most scientifically inclined of all the arms and services. Leaders in the Signal Corps, past and present—men like Adolphus Washington Greely, George Owen Squier, and their ilk—were nationally respected for their contributions to science. But surely it would have made more sense *doctrinally* to assign aircraft to the Cavalry.

Reflect a moment on the traditional doctrinal roles of Cavalry as a combat arm. First, there was the long-range, deep penetration *strategic mission*—strike the enemy homeland, disrupt transportation and communications, and burn factories. Next, there was the *screening mission* using the speed differential of the horse as compared with marching men to fan out in front and on the flanks to give a tripwire against enemy approaches and to conceal friendly concentrations. Third, there was the *interdiction mission*—attacks against the flanks of enemy columns before they can close with the friendly main battle force. Fourth, there was the *reconnaissance role*—serving as the eyes of the army, giving early warning of enemy moves to nullify surprise and reveal openings and opportunities for friendly initiatives. And finally, there was the *charge*, l'arme blanche, sabers raised, knee-to-knee, the impact weapon and shock action.

Aircraft, even in their crude and undeveloped state in the years before World War I, gave promise of becoming a far better

115

horse. Certainly insofar as reconnaissance, interdiction, and the strategic role were concerned, the airplane bid fair to replace the horse. But the cavalrymen would have none of it. They didn't like machinery—they loved horses. As a minister for war in Britain once put it, to ask cavalrymen to give up their horses was like asking a concert violinist to give up his instrument and use the gramophone.

I remember an old Cavalry recruiting poster on the wall outside my office when I was teaching at West Point. It proclaimed: "The Horse is Man's Noblest Companion." That says it all. Logic indicated that the airplane should be assigned to the Cavalry, a combat arm with its already well-defined and extensive range of missions and doctrine. But the human factor, the mindset of the cavalrymen dictated another solution. So aircraft were assigned to the Signal Corps, a *service* not a combat arm. And for a whole generation Billy Mitchell and others struggled to break out of the "service" mold and secure for the airmen not only an organization appropriate for its full doctrinal potential, but also to secure resources sufficient to implement that potential.

Has our organizational structure for space unwittingly fallen into the pattern that befell the airplane? Have we evolved our military space efforts as an ancillary *service* rather than as a combat arm? The language of those who speak knowledgeably on this subject and from positions of authority certainly reflects this perspective. We hear much of "mission support," an electronic bit stream providing the operating forces with pictures, words, weather reports, navigational signals, and the like, but only oblique and fleeting references to a combat role.[13] As an under secretary of the Air Force put it: "The United States has never had weapons of any kind deployed in space and currently has no approved programs for the deployment of such systems in orbit."[14]

Of course, it is entirely possible that those in command may feel constrained by our current treaty obligations or by a sincere desire to avoid stimulating a politically undesirable arms race. They may feel constrained to avoid discussing space vehicles in a combat role, whether as "space superiority fighters" or as offensive strategic weapons. But surely the history of the early air arm and its organizational misadventure should give us pause. When it comes to national defense, which in the final analysis means *national survival,* treaties can be modified or abrogated by the prescribed procedure if need be. At the very least, with the message of our own institutional past ringing in our ears, it behooves us to study the organizational problem of space with the utmost care.

From the Air Service–Air Corps–Air Force perspective, there would seem to be two pressing organizational issues confronting all of us who think about the military in space. We must decide on the contours and dimensions of the space command or space force, whichever it turns out to be. But first we must develop our space doctrine because the doctrine we decide upon will inexorably influence the structure of the space organization we build.

If air arm doctrine at the end of World War I still defined the principal function of aircraft as observation, then logically it made sense to establish an Air Service in the years immediately following as an adjunct, subordinate to and supporting the combat arms. If we define our role in space as "mission support" for the operating forces, then will it not logically follow that the organization we build for space will be appropriate for a service or support role? Will we then have to wait for some latter-day Billy Mitchell, some "space power" zealot, to buck the system and belatedly break out of the mold to develop a combat arm role for space?

Doctrine, especially space doctrine, is vitally important. But we are confronted with the old chicken and egg dilemma: Which comes first? Doctrine will shape organization, but, until we perfect our organization for devising space doctrine, it is doubtful if we will be able to formulate a thoroughly satisfactory doctrine for space. The work of perfecting doctrine is complex; it calls for the willing and *informed* cooperation of many participants. Indeed, it calls for the exercise of substantial initiatives by participants in all the operating echelons. It cannot be left exclusively to a handful of specialists in a staff section.

Consider, for a moment, the very real differences between doctrine, on the one hand, and research and development—R&D—on the other. There are powerful economic incentives behind R&D. In our free, competitive, capitalist system, eager contractors are forever pressing technological innovations upon us. Their exciting proposals always outstrip our resources and force us to make hard choices. Nonetheless, the zeal of the contractors in coming forward with ever more remarkable developments virtually ensures an almost exponential technological progress.

But what economic motive force is there behind the formulation of doctrine? Where we pour literally billions of dollars into R&D, into ever more advanced hardware, we consign the task of generating space doctrine to scarcely more than a handful of staff officers already laden with a multitude of other tasks. And to make matters worse, the record of promotions for officers so assigned has not been such as to stimulate any great surge of eager talent into this exacting and demanding work. Clearly, in the absence of strong economic incentives to perfect our space doctrine, we would be well advised not only to concoct a highly efficient structure, an organization, but also appropriate *procedures* for devising sound doctrinal ideas. If we fail to do this *now*—in the immediate future—will we not be doomed to flounder ineffectually within the constraints of an organizational structure geared to a conception of the space mission long since outgrown?

To escape such constraints, to reach beyond a service or support role in space, there are some among us who think they discern a clear "lesson" from history. They urge that we follow the historical example of the Air Force and seek doctrinal fulfillment through organizational autonomy in an entirely separate "Space Force." The parallels are admittedly striking. What is more, they can draw upon the wisdom of the past to sanction such a course. On the argument that the problems of the space environment are unique and fundamentally different from those of aircraft, the advocates of a space force can quote the great English scholar and statesman Thomas Babington Macaulay, who said, "it is an axiom in the science of organization, as in mechanics, that organizations or mechanisms designed to perform a double function rarely, if ever, perform either function satisfactorily."[15] But against this voice from the past, let me bring you another insight from history in the form of a revealing anecdote.

Some time after the Civil War when Gen Ulysses Grant was being lionized and honored as the architect of victory and the savior of the Union, a group of admirers raised a fund to express their appreciation by presenting him with a large collection of military history books for his enjoyment in retirement. Anxious not to waste money on duplicates, they asked General Grant to furnish them with a list of the military history volumes in his personal library. They were somewhat flummoxed when the hero replied that he didn't read any books on military history but had relied on a few simple principles and common sense. This anecdote merely highlights the point made by some perceptive scholars that many of the disasters of the Civil War might have been avoided if generals on both sides had been less diligent in reading Jomini's studies of Napoleonic warfare from which they drew "lessons" that subsequent advances in technology such as the railroad and the minié ball had made irrelevant or obsolete.[16]

What, then, should one carry away from this discourse? First, I hope you will realize that history is a seductive mistress. A superficial reading can lead us to answers that are plausible but unsound, so-called lessons of doubtful validity. History will serve us best when it is used to suggest questions that induce a profounder knowledge of the issues at stake. Secondly, should we follow the example of the Air Force and seek an autonomous space force? I wouldn't presume to pontificate with an answer to that complex question. But one can say with assurance: doctrine and organization are intricately and probably inextricably related. Therefore, if we wish to resolve our organizational problem in an enduring way, we will be well advised to address the doctrinal issue—and do so *now*. And in doing this we will be well advised if we pay more attention to the process and the procedures actually involved in formulating doctrine than we have hitherto.

Notes

1. Quoted in E. Ziemke, "Annihilation, Attrition and the Short War," *Parameters* 12 (March 1982), 23.

2. K. Booth, "History or Logic as Approaches to Strategy," Royal United Service Institute (RUSI) *Journal* 117 (September 1972): 38–39.

3. Jay Luvaas, "Military History: Is it still practicable," *Parameters* 12 (March 1982): 3, 5.

4. Robert H. Goddard, "A Method of Reaching Extreme Altitudes," Smithsonian Miscellaneous Collections 71, 1919.

5. Henry H. Arnold, *Infantry Journal* 10 (September 1913): 224–29.

6. Frederick D. Sturdee, "Changes in the Conditions of Naval Warfare Owing to the Introduction of the Ram, the Torpedo, and the Submarine Mine . . . ," RUSI *Journal* 30 (1886): 367–419.

7. *Journal of the US Infantry Association* 6 (July 1909): 84.

8. *Cavalry Journal* 20 (November 1909): 617. I am indebted to my student Capt John Bonin, author of a brilliant study of helicopter doctrine, for this and the foregoing citation.

9. P. R. Schratz, "The American Tradition of Dissent," *Shipmate* 38 (October 1975): 7. Also see Michael Vlahos, "A Crack in the Shield: the Capital Ship Concept Under Attack," *Journal of Strategic Studies* 2 (March 1979): 59.

10. Kenneth Werrell, *Evolution of the Cruise Missile: Yesterday, Today, and Tomorrow* (Maxwell Air Force Base, Ala.: Airpower Research Institute, 1981), 226.

11. Chief of the air service, AEF, "Final Report," *Air Service Information Circular* 2 (15 February 1921): 49.

12. Quoted in I. B. Holley, *Ideas and Weapons: Exploitation of the Aerial Weapon by the United States during World War II, A Study in the Relationship of Technological Advance, Military Doctrine, and the Development of Weapons* (New Haven: Yale University Press, 1953), 172.

13. See, for example, the excellent article by Lt Gen Richard C. Henry, "View from the Top," *Military Electronics/Countermeasures* 7 (July 1981): 13.

14. Under Secretary Edward C. Aldridge, "The New Space Command," Secretary of the Air Force, Office of Public Affairs, Washington, D.C., 22–26.

15. T. B. Macaulay, *History of England* (London: Macmillan 1913).

16. John G. Moore, "Mobility and Strategy in the Civil War," *Military Affairs* 24 (Summer 1960): 68.

Essay 9

A Modest Proposal:
Making Doctrine More Memorable*

On the subject of doctrine there are two problems. The first is to perfect the means for devising sound doctrine. The second is to perfect the means for ensuring that the doctrine we devise is communicated effectively to and internalized by the people who must apply it. I have spent the better part of my career in the Air Force trying to improve the process by which we formulate doctrine. In this I must confess I have been far from successful. But in recent months I have come to realize that the way we go about instilling doctrine in the minds of Air Force decision makers is no less important than the way we devise doctrine out of experience.

My thesis addresses the proposition that the way we articulate doctrine is flawed. My simple contention is that our doctrinal manuals consist largely of generalizations. They offer page after page of abstractions. Unfortunately, abstractions don't stick in the mind as well as real-life illustrations or historical examples. I contend that paying more attention to the format in which doctrine is presented will work toward a wider familiarity with doctrine by Air Force decision makers at all echelons.

Over the years, various strategies have been employed to ensure that Air Force officers become familiar with official doctrine. I suspect that few people recollect that 40 years ago we had a regulation requiring that each officer in the Air Force receive a personal copy of Air Force Manual (AFM) 1-1. This approach didn't work. It resulted in a lot of unread pamphlets and a mass of wastepaper. Some years later the doctrine shop staff tried another approach. They sought to lighten up the text with illustrations of Air Force thinkers to accompany quotations from their pronouncements. This effort was quickly

---

*This essay originated as a paper presented at a doctrine symposium held at the Center for Aerospace Doctrine, Research, and Education (CADRE) at the Air University, 19 April 1995. It was subsequently printed in *Airpower Journal* 9 (Winter 1995).

dismissed and consigned to oblivion when critics contemptuously called it the "comic strip" manual.

Then just last year [1994] at our doctrine symposium at Air University, Gen Michael Dugan tried another tack. He held up a 16-page pamphlet that constituted an early version of basic doctrine and admonished us to get back to that brief statement of the essentials. General Dugan's plea was further evidence that Air Force doctrine is not getting across as effectively as it should. Far too many officers still are not really familiar with the essence of our basic doctrine. General Dugan made a good try, but will brevity—going back to a 16-page document—do the trick? It didn't seem to work when we issued a personal copy of such a short pamphlet to every officer in the Air Force. Do we have any reason to think it will work any better today? I don't think so. This leads me to suggest my "modest proposal."

Why don't we experiment with a radical change in format and adopt a form of presentation that takes account of how the human mind works. Much experience has shown that we find it easier to recall specific examples—historical instances—than purely abstract generalizations. Accepting this reality, why don't we accompany every doctrinal idea with an illustrative example?

Consider an architectural analogy for building and disseminating doctrine as shown in table 1. At the top of column 1 is the frieze—the band at the top of the wall. The wall itself is the wainscoting, and down at the bottom is the baseboard. Now let's apply these divisions to the format I propose (column 2).

Table 1

Doctrinal Model

Architectural Analogy	Proposed Format
Frieze	Doctrine
Wainscoting	Historical illustration
Baseboard	Footnote to sources

The frieze will be a statement of doctrine. The wainscoting will provide an example—a historical illustration of the doctrinal idea. And down at the baseboard, we have a citation showing the archival or published source of the historical illustration.

In addition to the source citation for the illustrative example, there should be other citations leading to other similar examples and instances. Additional citations provide several advantages. Their mere presence indicates that the people who formulated the doctrinal statement at the top of the page didn't generalize from a single example but rested the doctrine on a broad range of experience. Further, the additional citations would guide instructors in our staff and war colleges to persuasive illustrations in support of the doctrines they are teaching.

Now, let me illustrate the format proposed here with an actual example (table 2). The doctrinal statement is a generalization, an abstraction. It goes back to Clausewitz's famous dictum that *"war is nothing but the continuation of policy with other means"* (emphasis in original).[1] But standing alone, how much of an impression does it make? However, when we go to

Table 2

Illustrative Example 1

Doctrinal statement: "War is an instrument of political policy." AFM 1-1, *Basic Aerospace Doctrine of the United States Air Force,* vol. 1, March 1992, 1.

Historical illustration: "US military planners seriously underestimated the impact that Scud attacks would have on the overall political situation. They recognized that militarily Scuds were insignificant; they were inaccurate, had a small payload, etc. The military planners' failure was in not foreseeing the political impact. The political need to keep the Coalition together and seriousness of the Israeli threat to retaliate unilaterally quickly resulted in a military impact on the air campaign in that a significant amount of the most capable elements of USAF forces had to be diverted to 'Scud Hunting' missions. The political need to react to the Scuds overrode the military desire to keep the tactical plan on track."

Citation: *Gulf War Air Power Survey,* vol. 1, *Planning and Command and Control* (Washington, D.C.: Government Printing Office, 1993), pt. 1, 102–4.

the historical example, we meet a real-life event—an application of the doctrinal notion. Here, it is easy to see that there are times when the demands of the political situation override well-established doctrinal verities such as the top priority of the need to gain air superiority.

Other examples come readily to mind. For instance, one might use the sinking of the *Lusitania* by a German U-boat in World War I as a negative illustration. The *Lusitania* was carrying munitions, and it was in a war zone, so it was technically a legitimate target. But if German policy was to avoid bringing the United States into the war on the Allied side, then sinking the *Lusitania* was a strategic mistake.

Let's look at another example. During the Gulf War of 1991, our strategic planners followed sound doctrine in attacking the command structure of the Iraqi forces. Decapitating enemy command and control pays high dividends. To this end, our air strikes hit the Al Firdos bunker. As it turned out, large numbers of civilians were killed in the process. Saddam charged us with wantonly attacking a civilian bomb shelter. The photograph in the New York Times showing iron-barred gates on the bunker certainly gave the lie to his claim. Apparently, the officers assigned to the command bunker had invited their families to join them there, believing that the hardened bunker was one of the safest places in Baghdad. They were mistaken.

The high loss of civilian lives, however, had its impact in the United States. Fighting a war with Cable News Network looking over your shoulder has its difficulties. Ever sensitive to public opinion and the need to sustain popular support for the war, high-level decision makers, probably Gen Colin Powell or Gen Norman Schwarzkopf, promptly intruded on the target-selection process and thereafter withheld most targets in the Baghdad area—another example of political concern overriding purely military considerations.[2]

In my first example, the suggested innovative format goes all the way back to Clausewitz. Another illustration reflects a much more recent instance of a doctrinal notion (table 3).[3] Once again, I have deliberately shortened the historical statement for simplicity.

Table 3

Illustrative Example 2

Doctrinal statement: "Strategic attacks are defined by objective—not by the weapon system employed, munition used, or target location." AFM 1-1, *Basic Aerospace Doctrine of the United States Air Force,* vol. 1, March 1992, 11.
Historical illustration: "For many years the Air Force has painted itself into a strategic-tactical paradigm that was artificially based on platforms and weapons instead of objectives. Desert Storm demonstrated that this paradigm was flawed. Single-seat 'fighters' (F-117) carried out textbook strategic attacks on the enemy capital; single-seat, close-air-support aircraft (A-10s) carried out anti-Scud operations with grave strategic and political implications, while the world's premier 'strategic' bomber (B-52) bombed mine fields protecting the enemy's frontline trenches. The growing realization of the 'indivisibility of air power' was part and parcel of the unification of the Air Force's two combat organizations, SAC and TAC in the Air Combat Command."
Citation: *Gulf War Air Power Survey,* vol. 5, *A Statistical Compendium and Chronology* (Washington, D.C.: Government Printing Office, 1993), pt. 1, tables 177 and 185, 418 and 517.

My proposal for a radical revision of format—the way we present doctrine—is offered as an experiment. It may well fail to accomplish a greater understanding and familiarity with doctrine throughout the Air Force. But, given the perception that we have not been very successful in communicating doctrine in our various previous publications since World War II, it would appear that a change in format may well be worth a try. One of the side effects of the change in format I'm advocating is the impact it should have on credibility. If doctrine writers are required to document each doctrinal statement with several citations to specific historical experience, then surely their generalizations will be more believable and more readily acceptable to the reader. Anyone who wishes to dispute the validity of the doctrinal generalization must assume the burden of proof by digging up contrary examples.

In the past, when proposed or draft manuals were circulated to the major commands for comment, the responses were of two types. Either the commands returned a perfunctory approval, which suggests that little or no really serious thought had been given to the details, or they raised violent objections to one or more features of the proposed doctrinal text. Disagreement can lead to a healthy dialectic and exchange of ideas on the merits of the case, but not infrequently these objections have been raised without accompanying historical evidence to justify the objection. So it is my contention that requiring doctrine writers at all echelons to support their formulations with citations to actual experience will not only improve credibility but will impose a higher level of objectivity on people who wish to dispute any given doctrinal statement.

Now I want to circle back to the place where I began. I suggested that we have two basic problems with doctrine: (1) to perfect the means for devising sound doctrine, and (2) to perfect the means for ensuring that the doctrine we devise is communicated effectively and is successfully internalized by those who must apply it.

Let's turn now to the task of devising sound doctrine. Little wonder that we are still groping in our efforts to improve the way we formulate doctrine. Although informal doctrinal writings have existed since remote antiquity, the phenomenon of formal, officially sanctioned and periodically revised or updated doctrines is of comparatively recent date. The famous British military historian G. F. R. Henderson, writing in 1905, put it this way: "In the British Army no means existed for collecting, much less analyzing, the facts and phenomena of the battlefield and the range. Experience was regarded as the private property of individuals, not as a public asset to be applied to the benefit of the army as a whole. . . . The suggestion that a branch should be established for that purpose . . . was howled down."[4]

We have come a long way since Henderson wrote those words, but we are still far from having perfected the means by which we formulate doctrine. We talk about jointness, yet to this day the way the Navy defines and describes doctrine is quite different from the way the Air Force and the Army define it. To my utter dismay, a chairman of the Joint Chiefs of Staff displayed a different conception of doctrine from the prevailing Air Force view. After the tragic-shoot down of the friendly helicopters in Iraq, the chairman, in an effort to avoid a repetition of this unfortunate episode, proposed to *mandate* certain doctrinal procedures.[5] He did this in spite of the fact that much effort over many years has been expended in trying to make absolutely clear that officially promulgated doctrine is *never* prescriptive, *never* mandatory, and *never* rigidly binding on the commander in the field. It is only suggestive. Doctrine is only what has usually worked best in the past. It never curtails a commander's freedom of action. If doctrine ever becomes mandatory, it will curb initiative and lead to lockstep performance—if it is not ignored entirely.

Not only do wide differences exist in the way we interpret the term *doctrine*—indeed the very concept of doctrine—but also today we have no clearly defined and established procedures for compiling doctrinal manuals. Although none of us doubts that the USAF is the best air force in the world, that fact should not deter us from learning whatever we can from the air arms of other nations.

Some time ago, some of our friends in the Royal Australian Air Force (RAAF) sent me the published proceedings of what they termed a Regional Air Power Workshop held in Darwin in August 1993. It includes a chapter devoted to the development of doctrine. What immediately caught my eye were two brief lists.

The first was captioned "We want doctrine to"

- reveal capabilities of air forces yet offer guidance on how best to use those capabilities;

- be enduring yet flexible (i.e., be valid over time yet responsive to change);

- provide guidance to personnel yet remain open to interpretation;

- provide direction yet not be too restrictive;

- guide research and development yet adjust to technological innovations; and

- set out maxims and imperatives.

I'm not suggesting that we ought to copy these verbatim, but it strikes me that such a presentation as an introduction to our manual might be helpful. The second list followed the heading "Doctrine offers"

- a conceptual framework;

- general guidance in specific situations;

- a foundation for the air force (including force structure, strategy, tactics, training, and procedures);

- guidance for establishing employment priorities;

- a sounding board for testing, evaluating, and employing new technologies and new policies; and

- a rationale for the organization and employment of air forces.[6]

One may argue that there's little that is new here, but the point I'm trying to make is that it is useful to spell these ideas out in our doctrinal manuals by way of introduction to the newcomers.

If we are going to spell out the procedures for devising doctrine, we have to start with the three well-known potential sources.

1. Theory: the visionary speculations of individuals of unusual imagination. Theories and visions can be helpful in virtually forcing us to appreciate possibilities that most of us have overlooked. But theories are hypothetical, and they lack the substance of reality—the test of actual trial.

2. Technological advance: the significant breakthrough that opens up a whole new range of tactical possibilities. Sometimes doctrine *pushes* the creation of a technological advance, and sometimes an unexpected technological breakthrough *pulls* doctrine into a new and unanticipated arena. A good example is the case of US power plant production in World War II. As world leaders in the development of piston engines, our designers kept pushing the envelope with bigger and bigger piston engines. This effort culminated in a gargantuan, multirow radial by Lycoming, now on display at the Silver Hill facility of the Smithsonian Air and Space Museum. It was an obsolete dinosaur the day it was finished because a visionary designer named Whittle developed, on a financial

shoestring, a revolutionary jet engine that induced significant doctrinal changes.

3. Day-to-day operations of the Air Force in peace as well as in war: the major source of doctrine. Major technological breakthroughs are important stimuli to doctrinal change but they are far from the commonest cause of such changes. Daily operations are the source I want to consider now.

Historical experience provides the proof of what has worked and what has not worked. Experience carries us beyond the visions and speculations of theorists. Actual experience reveals that which is practical. But what do we really mean by experience? Living through an operation is in one sense "experiencing it." However, that is not what we mean by *usable experience for doctrinal purposes.* To be usable, the experience we observe or live through has to be reflected upon and *recorded.* Recording is a demanding task for it involves explicating the context in which the experience was acquired—the prevailing conditions, institutions, equipment, and the like.

Without thoughtful reflection, careful analysis, and objective *recording,* experience is almost meaningless. Frederick the Great recognized this problem. "Some of my pack mules," he said, "have experienced three campaigns, but they still don't know anything about waging war." We have able and talented officers in the doctrine shop in the Pentagon and at the Air Force Doctrine Center collocated with the Air University at Maxwell Air Force Base, Alabama, as well as in other echelons of the Air Force, but they are utterly dependent upon the historical experience of the Air Force at large to provide them with the evidence, the case histories, and the after-action reports that provide the substance of doctrine.

I've been working the doctrinal problem for nearly 50 years, and my observation is that the weak link in the process of generating doctrine is the paucity of well-prepared after-action reports. If the people who are charged with formulating doctrine have only a few cases upon which to base the generalizations that we call doctrine, then almost certainly their inferences are going to be skewed.

Doctrine is everybody's business in the Air Force. We have never sold that idea. Perhaps we should come up with a system of incentives for the most useful after-action reports produced each year. Our Canadian army friends have tackled the problem head-on. They established the *Canadian Army Training and Doctrine Bulletin* as a vehicle to circulate new doctrine and to provide a forum for the discussion of ideas that have not reached the status of formal doctrine. This strikes me as a good idea, but if our existing professional journals are doing their job properly, then surely the discussion of doctrinal ideas ought to take a large place in their pages.

Although I have indicated that our collective experience—properly recorded and communicated for people assigned to formulate official doctrine—should be a major component of doctrine, we certainly don't mean to suggest that past experience is an infallible guide to future action. That's why we say that doctrine is advisory, suggestive, and not mandatory. As Mark Twain put it, "history doesn't exactly repeat itself, but it rhymes."

Notes

1. Carl von Clausewitz, *On War*, ed. and trans. Michael Howard and Peter Paret (Princeton, N.J.: Princeton University Press, 1976), 69.

2. Col Edward C. Mann III, *Thunder and Lightning: Desert Storm and the Airpower Debates* (Maxwell AFB, Ala.: Air University Press, April 1995), 157–58.

3. I am indebted to my former student, Lt Col Dan Kuehl, USAF, retired, currently on the faculty of the National Defense University for the two doctrinal illustrations offered here.

4. G. F. R. Henderson, *The Science of War* (London: Longmans, 1905), 418–19.

5. Gen John Shalikashvili, chairman, Joint Chiefs of Staff, memorandum CM-367-94 and enclosure to Gen Merrill A. McPeak, chief of staff of the Air Force et al., 18 July 1994.

6. Gary Waters and John Mordike, eds., *Regional Air Power Workshop: Darwin* (Canberra, ACT, Australia: Air Power Studies Centre, 1993), 43–44.

Essay 10

Fifty Questions for Doctrine Writers: Means Are as Important as Ends*

Let me begin with a historical analogy. Early in his career, when he served as a congressman from Illinois, Abraham Lincoln was confronted with the necessity of voting for or against the declaration of war against Mexico in 1846. Ever the high-minded idealist, he voted against declaring war. It was, he said, an immoral land grab. His constituents thought differently. They saw the war as an ideal opportunity to expand the territory of the United States. So they voted him out of office.

Lincoln never forgot that lesson. He came to realize that idealism must always be tempered with realism and practicality. He came to realize that the workable way was a case of "eyes on the stars, feet on the ground." During the Civil War, for example, he wanted to free the slaves. But when he issued the Emancipation Proclamation, he excluded all those slaves held in states such as Maryland, which sided with the Union. Lincoln needed the votes and the manpower of those states to wage war effectively against the Confederacy. So the Emancipation Proclamation was a compromise. In the eyes of many abolitionist critics, it was a seriously flawed document—a sell-out. The only slaves it "freed" were those behind the Confederate lines—the very ones the Union forces didn't yet control. But as we now know, though flawed and compromised, the proclamation worked.

What am I trying to say here? The means we employ when we undertake to formulate doctrine are every bit as important as the ends we seek. The ends we seek are implicit in the means we use. That is one of the fundamental philosophical

*This essay was originally presented as a lecture at a symposium sponsored by the Center for Airpower Doctrine, Research, and Education (CADRE) and subsequently published as an article in *Airpower Journal* (Fall 1997). I wish to acknowledge the contribution of my former graduate student, Maj Robert Taguchi, USA, who propounded a checklist for doctrine writers at my urging, which I found helpful in preparing this article.

principles that undergird this great republic in which we live. I repeat: the ends we seek are implicit in the means we use.

I have devoted much of my professional life in the Air Force to the quest for suitable air doctrine. I have written books and articles for this purpose. It now appears that my efforts have been without much success for we are still groping for a better path to sound doctrine. Our procedures for devising doctrine at all echelons are still far from ideal. Look about you. Do we anywhere have a comprehensive set of instructions to guide those people who are assigned the difficult task of producing Air Force doctrine?

I propose to ask a series of searching questions to help those people who are launching a new doctrinal center at Air University. First, what should we ask about the composition of the team, the officers selected to formulate doctrine for the Air Force? What past experience and education uniquely qualify them for this duty? In prior assignments, have they given evidence of creative imagination? Have they demonstrated a capacity for rigorous evaluation of conflicting evidence? Does the doctrine team reflect an adequate spectrum of experience to cope with the whole range of potential Air Force capabilities?

Next, are doctrine writers employing adequate procedures in gathering evidence on air arm experience to formulate sound doctrine? Do they cast their research net widely enough? Do they survey the fullest possible range of after-action reports and similar sources from the field? If after-action reports are a primary source of air arm operational experience, have doctrine writers taken steps to ensure that the scope and quality of such reports are adequate for doctrinal purposes? Are after-action reports as objective as they ought to be? In the view of this observer, very little is currently being done to enhance the quality of such reports and the regularity with which they are submitted.

Has the doctrine team comprehensively studied the experience of foreign air forces? Has it guarded against the bias that arises from relying only on those reports of foreign experience and practice that have been translated, while ignoring contrary evidence that happens not to have been translated? Has appropriate account been taken of cultural or material differences underlying foreign experience and practice when weighing the utility of foreign doctrinal ideas?

What can we learn from the ways and means employed by foreign air forces in formulating doctrine? Has our doctrine team ever undertaken any systematic effort along this line? Do foreign air forces have procedural manuals or regulations on the formulation of doctrine that might offer us insights on their methods, if not their doctrines? In recent years, I have been much impressed with the way the Royal Australian Air Force (RAAF) has grappled with the problem of doctrine. A small air force with limited funding, the RAAF has been driven to think deeply about doctrinal issues. Has the USAF studied this source in depth?

Before publishing USAF official doctrine, what steps should doctrine writers undertake to test the validity of their formulations? Have they launched "trial balloons" in the form of journal articles to elicit feedback? How successful is the practice of holding symposia in developing new or revised doctrine? Does the current practice of circulating drafts to the Air Force major commands (MAJCOM) for comment elicit constructive replies? Do the MAJCOMs evaluate proposed doctrine comprehensively? Or do they respond critically only when some vested interest of the command seems threatened? Has the doctrine team undertaken a systematic survey of knowledgeable individuals to supplement the written record of after-action reports and other such evidence? Has it been at pains to interview individuals at all echelons—not just senior officers—to secure the widest possible perspective on a given body of experience? What steps should be taken to prepare interviewers to elicit objective evidence? Are the interviewers sensitive to the danger of asking, wittingly or unwittingly, leading questions that elicit the answers desired—answers that conform to their presuppositions? Do doctrine writers have adequate funding to permit the travel that might be required to elicit the kind of testimony needed—especially that of junior participants with actual operational experience?

Have doctrine writers paid appropriate heed to support functions, or have their efforts been almost exclusively devoted to operational concerns? Doctrine applies to logistics as well as tactics. Do we have suitable logistical doctrine? Do we have suitable research and development doctrine? At a time when preserving the industrial base is an acute problem, what guidance can doctrine suggest? This nation has experienced earlier and even more drastic reductions in defense spending that have savaged the industrial base. What generalized experience from such past history can inform our doctrine writers today?

When doctrine writers assess success or failure in past operations, do they ask if flawed performance or faulty doctrine led to failure? Can extant doctrine be effectively evaluated without a conscious awareness of many other factors that may have contributed to success or failure? Will the same or similar "other factors" be present when our current doctrine is applied?

What have been the sources of significant doctrinal innovation in the past? Will a study of such patterns of innovation lead to a prompter development of appropriate doctrine? Because technological advances are a major factor in forcing doctrinal revision, what procedures should doctrinal writers establish to ensure an adequate response to "on-the-horizon" technologies?

Given that all thinkers and writers are subtly influenced by their assumptions, wittingly or unwittingly, what steps should doctrine writers take to ensure that their assumptions are valid? Should doctrine writers reach outside their immediate organization to invite critical evaluations of their assumptions to avoid parochial bias? Should some such outside critics be drawn from the other military services or even foreign services?

Beyond probing our assumptions, what steps should the doctrine team take to test the validity of its formulations? Beyond feedback from various Air Force echelons, what actual field testing should be undertaken in peacetime via maneuvers, exercises, and the like? Have the doctrine folk established effective liaison with such ongoing operations as Red Flag? Should doctrine writers solicit high command support for more far-reaching testing of key doctrinal formulations?

Should our doctrine team give thought to what is now often referred to as asymmetrical hostile actions? Does the Air Force have a valid role in countering terrorism? If so, then surely we must spell out suitable doctrine for dealing with such threats. And what about nonviolent terrorism or economic mischief making? In 1995 a Russian hacker in Saint Petersburg broke into Citicorp's computerized cash management system in New York and capriciously transferred $12 million to various banks around the world. The Russian police cooperated with the FBI in apprehending this scoundrel, but what he did may have been a blessing in alerting us to the potential for such nonviolent acts of terrorism.[1] I'm not convinced that the Air Force has a role or a responsibility in confronting such threats. I mention them only to suggest that our doctrine writers must decide what threats require a doctrinal response.

Have our doctrine writers given adequate attention to the means by which doctrine is promulgated or disseminated? Are doctrine manuals the best way to communicate doctrine? Do manuals as now conceived employ the most effective format?[2] What alternative or supplemental means of promulgating, communicating, or distributing doctrinal ideas might we employ to ensure greater circulation and penetration within the officer corps?

Today the Air Force is much concerned over cooperating with people engaged in developing joint doctrine. To what extent does human nature operate to inhibit the successful application of joint doctrine? All military organizations need to achieve cohesion—the bonding of members in a given service. But such bonding tends to generate a "them versus us" outlook, which is detrimental to jointness. Does our Air Force organizational culture thus adversely influence the practice, if not the words, of joint doctrine?[3]

Can writers of joint doctrine overcome the inherent differences that exist, for example, between the ground-arm perspective and the air-arm perspective? Whereas the ground folk stress coordination, we stress flexibility. As my friend Roger Spiller of the Army Command and General Staff College once asked, is the search for joint doctrine "a continuing process of negotiation and reconciliation between interests" the object of which is "the triumph of one over the other?" Can we devise ways to overcome this parochial service rivalry? Must those people who negotiate joint doctrine always regard concessions as "giving up the farm"—a surrender of control? Does the personality of individuals who negotiate the formulation of joint

135

doctrine make a critical difference? If so, what considerations should enter in the selection of such negotiators?

One might go on proliferating a hundred more questions of the sort I have already posed. But now let me consider other approaches to the problem of improving the ways we generate doctrine. Gen Donn Starry, one of the ablest thinkers of the Army, now retired, a dozen or so years ago wrote an article entitled "To Change an Army," which offers some provocative guidelines that should be of interest as we go about developing a new approach to doctrine writing.[4]

General Starry, who toward the end of his career headed the Army's Training and Doctrine Command (TRADOC), asked, "what are the factors required to effect change?" This I take to mean, "what does it require to introduce significant new doctrine?" This he follows with a checklist that strongly suggests that promulgating doctrine involves far more than publishing a manual. Let's look at the steps he offers:

- There must be an institution or mechanism to identify the need for change, to draw up parameters for change, and to describe clearly what is to be done and how that differs from what has been done before.

- The educational background of the principal staff and command personalities responsible for change must be sufficiently rigorous, demanding, and relevant to bring a common cultural bias to the solution of problems.

- There must be a spokesman for change. The spokesman can be a person, one of the mavericks; an institution such as a staff college; or a staff agency.

- Whoever or whatever it may be, the spokesman must build a consensus that will give the new ideas, and the need to adopt them, a wider audience of converts and believers.

- There must be continuity among the architects of change so that consistency of effort is brought to bear on the process.

- Someone at or near the top of the institution must be willing to hear out arguments for change, agree to the need, embrace the new operational concepts, and become at least a supporter, if not a champion, of the cause for change.

- Changes proposed must be subjected to trials. Their relevance must be convincingly demonstrated to a wide audience by experiment and experience, and necessary modifications must be made as a result of such trial outcomes.[5]

We would do well to reflect on these suggestions as we perfect the new doctrinal center at Air University.

Finally, I want to turn from the doctrinal writers and their problems of procedure and organization to consider the recipients—the readers and users of doctrine. Do Air Force officers understand what doctrine really is? Do they know what the intended use of doctrine is? Does the Air Force in its whole system of professional military education (PME) ever explicitly instruct officers in the proper use of doctrine? I suspect not when we hear a senior flag officer asserting that doctrine is "bull crap."

Can we improve our PME to achieve a better understanding, Air Force-wide, of what doctrine is and is not? Surely this should be one of the initiatives of the new doctrinal center. Doctrine is not and was never meant to be prescriptive. Doctrine is suggestive. It says, "this is what has usually worked best in the past," but this in no way frees decision makers from the need to form their own judgment in any given situation. If the study of war tells us anything, it is that the only constant is war's inconstancy—that it is filled with surprises, contingencies, and unknowns.

We have seriously neglected educating our officers in how to read doctrine and how to use it. Well-educated officers must engage in a critical intellectual activity, with the doctrinal options available to them. Doctrines are not a series of universally valid maxims or positive prescriptions. They are points of departure for the thoughtful decision maker, who must judge each situation individually. When we say doctrine is "authoritative," all we mean is that it is objectively recorded experience that remains worthy of and requires the critical attention of the decision maker.

Notes

1. Timothy L. Thomas, "Deterring Information Warfare: A New Strategic Challenge," *Parameters* 26, no. 4 (Winter 1996–1997): 81.

2. Maj Gen I. B. Holley Jr., "A Modest Proposal: Making Doctrine More Memorable," *Airpower Journal* 9, no. 4 (Winter 1995): 14–20.

3. R. S. Parkin, "The Goodwill of the Services and the Problems of the Lesser Partner: The Creation of the Australian Manual of Direct Air Support, 8 June 1942," Paper no. 42 (RAAF Base Fairbairn: RAAF Air Power Studies Centre, March 1997).

4. Gen Donn A. Starry, "To Change an Army," *Military Review* 63, no. 3 (March 1983): 20–27.

5. Ibid., 23.

Essay 11

The Dynamics of Doctrinal Development*

This essay tells a story—a case history, a historical example to illustrate what doctrine is all about; it traces a sequence of steps and defines some important terms to explain how doctrine is developed; and it suggests what needs to be done to improve the doctrinal process in the armed forces of the present day.

First, the case study: Doesn't it seem strange that the Union Army, with all the industrial resources of the Northern States at its back, fought virtually the entire Civil War with muzzle-loading rifles? The federal government enrolled 2,666,999 men in the armed forces in a desperate effort—including bribes in the form of enlistment bounties—to increase its firepower.[1] If Lincoln's administration had diverted even a small part of the resources put into rounding up warm bodies into developing rapid-fire, breech-loading weapons, which were already on the technological horizon though unperfected, far fewer Union troops would have been required to bring the war to a success-ful conclusion for the North.

The development of rapid-fire weapons was certainly not be-yond the reach of the technology then in hand; the Spencer re-peating rifle, to take but one example, was available to the Union forces and was actually issued in substantial numbers toward the end of the war. What is more, Dr. Richard J. Gatling's machine-gun, patented in 1862 and tested by the Army Ordnance Department in 1863, offered even more excit-ing possibilities for developing superior firepower far beyond anything that could be obtained by adding more riflemen to the regimental front.[2]

My thesis is simple: the failure of the Union Army in the 1860s was not *technological but doctrinal;* the military leaders of the day failed to think all the way through the problem of

---

*This chapter is a substantially revised version of a lecture originally delivered in 1975 at the Air War College, Maxwell AFB, Alabama, and subsequently to nine other audiences at various institutions—Army, Navy, and Air Force.

firepower. By way of historical illustration one has only to follow the progress of the machine-gun in the US Army. Admittedly, the Gatling gun of 1863 was a crude affair with many shortcomings. It was hopper fed and hand crank operated. It had eight barrels because every previous attempt to design a rapid-fire weapon had foundered upon the technical limitation of overheating which jammed the breech mechanism.

In spite of many difficulties, successive improvements in design led to the development of a model so promising that despite declining appropriations, in 1867 the Ordnance Department procured 150 Gatlings—a real "production order"—for issue to the Army. But to what branch of the Army should the new weapon be assigned? Here the problem of doctrine comes into focus. Because of its eight barrels, the Gatling was excessively heavy. It required a rather massive carriage and sturdy wheels to sustain its weight; its limber* was so heavy it required horses to transport it across country. In short, the Gatling looked like an artillery piece, so it was assigned to the Field Artillery in the US Army.

Unfortunately for the future of rapid-fire weapons, at this juncture, in 1870, the Franco-Prussian war broke out. The French had developed a machine-gun of their own. Like the US Army, the French, too, had assigned it to the field artillery; they employed a number of these machine-guns against their Prussian foes—with disastrous results. Whenever the French machine-guns were pitted against the conventional field pieces of the Prussians in counterbattery duels, the greater range of conventional artillery tipped the scales in favor of the Germans. As a consequence, the machine-gun emerged from the war with a bad reputation. Only a few observers recognized that the weapon had been misused and that the *problem was doctrinal, not technological.*

Back in the United States, the years after 1870 afforded few occasions to test the utility of the Gatlings. The operational experience of the Army was for the most part confined to a series of Indian wars where large bodies of men were seldom encountered on either side, though one suspects Custer and his men at the Battle of Little Big Horn may have fervently

---

*A two-wheeled cart for transporting a caisson or gun

wished they had been equipped with Gatlings as the Indians closed in on them for the kill. Not surprisingly, doctrinal studies languished. Not until the Spanish-American War did the machine-gun emerge from a generation of neglect.

In 1898 a brash but imaginative infantry captain named John Henry Parker saw an opportunity to win fame and promotion for himself by advancing an idea he had long espoused. He talked Maj Gen William Shafter, the commanding general of the expedition to Cuba, into letting him organize a free-standing battery of machine-guns to support the infantry; then he wrangled his way onto the transports with his guns and gun crews before the expedition sailed out of Tampa. In Cuba, Parker pushed his machine-guns up to the front in the assault at Santiago, providing effective supporting fire for Teddy Roosevelt and his Rough Riders, thus acquiring a potential political ally for future advantage. Aspiring young officers may infer from this that it is well to exert oneself on behalf of a future president whenever possible!

Upon returning to the United States, Captain Parker hastily wrote a book trumpeting the virtues of the machine-gun, urging the creation of an independent corps, not unlike the Field Artillery, made up entirely of machine-guns and the troops to man them. His plan called for a brigadier general at the head of this new arm of the service. Needless to say, he hoped to be awarded that position himself. Unfortunately for Captain Parker's dreams of instant promotion to flag rank, he made some disparaging remarks about the effectiveness of the Field Artillery in his book expounding the merits of the machine-gun. Feelings were hurt, charges were leveled, there was in investigation, and Parker suffered a reprimand. Whatever adverse effects the impact of this imbroglio had on the career of John Henry Parker, the ensuing publicity did a great deal for the machine-gun, which thereafter received the tests and trials it deserved to make it a highly important infantry weapon.

Why tell this story about an episode that happened before the advent of the tank and the airplane, and before radar and so many other weapons in the present day arsenal? Precisely because it does antedate these weapons. Which is to say, most of the lessons one needs to know about the interplay of weapons and doctrine can be learned from the historical study of technological advances that eventuated in armament long before the appearance of the airplane, the missile, the spacecraft, or any other advanced form of modern weaponry. With this in mind it will be useful to turn to a consideration of the steps by which weapon systems are developed and then employed. In so doing it should be possible to distil out the bare essentials of the doctrinal process. Time enough later on to add in qualifications to take account of special cases and complexities. First, one must comprehend the process, the procedures, by which doctrine is formulated.

To begin with, one must understand the terminology. In the diagram below (fig. 2) there are four terms lying along a continuum, a spectrum, from left to right, all stemming initially from a physical event labeled *action* and moving on up through successive levels of awareness. This action could be an infantryman wielding a muzzle-loader, an Air Force pilot flying an F-15, or, for that matter, almost any of the transactions that take place in the armed forces, whether or not any hardware or weaponry is involved.

Action⟶Observer⟶Concept⟶Doctrine⟶Principles

Figure 2. Doctrine Continuum

The next step along the continuum after the action itself is the *observer*, that perceptive individual who not only sees the action, along with many of his contemporaries who may also be present, but unlike them draws an inference from his observation. This inference he proceeds to discipline by reducing it to writing. In doing so, the thoughtful observer formulates a concept.

Consider the term *concept;* what does it really mean? An original idea? Yes, but also something more. A concept is a working hypothesis, a tentative idea, a conceptualization, a way of visualizing a problem by expressing it in words. To be fully effective a concept must be articulated as a written formulation. The mere act of putting an idea into words compels precision, forces one to recognize nuances and differences. The more one gropes for precision and definition, the more one is forced to appreciate that the idea is still admittedly tentative, still subject to trial and error. It is precisely this uncertainty, this tentative quality, which differentiates a concept from the term *doctrine,* the next step along the continuum.

Doctrine is from the Latin *doctrina,* hence doctrine is literally "that which is taught." In traditional parlance, doctrine can best be described as distilled experience, generalized rules for employment, an agreed upon "best way" of doing something. Doctrines are suggested procedures for meeting recurring problems, procedures that have been officially approved for dissemination. The term *doctrine,* then, is heavily laden with the notion of accumulated experience, the tried and true. In contrast, the term *concept* bespeaks novelty, originality, and a venturing into the unknown, an imaginative conceptualization freshly created.

Going still further along the continuum, one comes to the highest level of distillation in the term *principles.* In military parlance, when one speaks of the principles of war the reference is to those elements of doctrine that have proved to be so enduring, so generally applicable, so universal, as to become virtually axiomatic, so widely accepted as to need no further sanction or proof. In the eighteenth century, Thomas Jefferson would have called them "self-evident truths." Against the spectrum of terms on the continuum we can return to the historical example, the case of the machine-gun in the US Army, with more insight.

One doesn't need much imagination to recognize what a miserably poor weapon the muzzle-loader was in the search for superior firepower. Trying to load, prime, and wield a ramrod in the heat of battle must have been a nerve-wracking business. One painfully revealing bit of Civil War evidence found on the battlefield at Petersburg makes this only too clear: a musket with 14 balls and powder charges rammed into the muzzle one on top of the other after the first load, all unnoticed by the infantryman in the heat of battle, had failed to fire![3]

Here, then, is action perceived by an observer: the muzzle-loading musket is an awkward and inadequate weapon. Dr. Gatling, for example, observes the action and makes an imaginative leap to draw an inference, coming up with an original idea, an alternative solution to the problem of generating battlefield firepower, a novel concept, the rapid-fire, breech-loading weapon. So this imaginative inventor-designer dreams up a hardware requirement, which is to say, he defines a set of performance specifications and designs the mechanisms to attain a workable machine-gun. One need not recount all the mechanical difficulties inevitably encountered as the inventor-designer struggles to eliminate one bug after another. When his workable prototype model is tested and reveals flaws, it is improved by a succession of modifications, each subjected to test and trial, until, belatedly, in 1867, Dr. Gatling is ready with a true production model to be manufactured in quantity.

The diagram in figure 3 traces the developmental process. The observer of each successive action draws an inference from what he observes, formulates a concept that is then fleshed out in actual hardware, moving from prototype through a succession of modifications to the production model. As soon as the new weapon has been shown to be technically feasible and is ready for issue to the troops, a whole new set of problems arise. The hardware requirement inexorably imposes a *procedural requirement*. Military users must not only make decisions as to what organization will employ the new weapon but must also begin to devise tactics and techniques appropriate for the fullest possible exploitation of its capabilities.

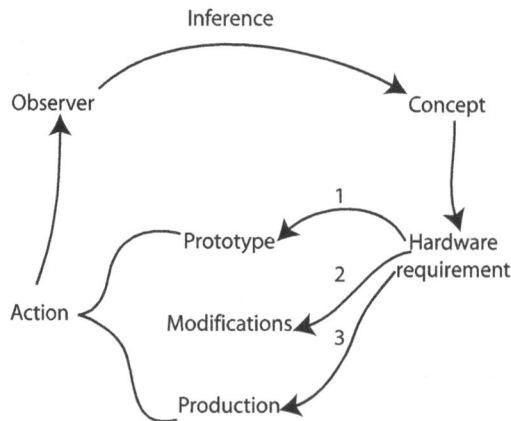

Figure 3. Doctrine Development Process

Figure 4 illustrates the cycle by which procedures are per-fected. Unfortunately, in the period between 1867 when the Gatling entered production and World War I, the military au-thorities did not think out all the ramifications of this process. Thus, they blundered about for nearly 50 years before they de-vised suitable tactics and techniques for employing the machine-gun with optimal effectiveness. From our present-day perspec-tive, however, we can identify several rather distinct stages in the formulation of tactics and techniques that become doctrine.

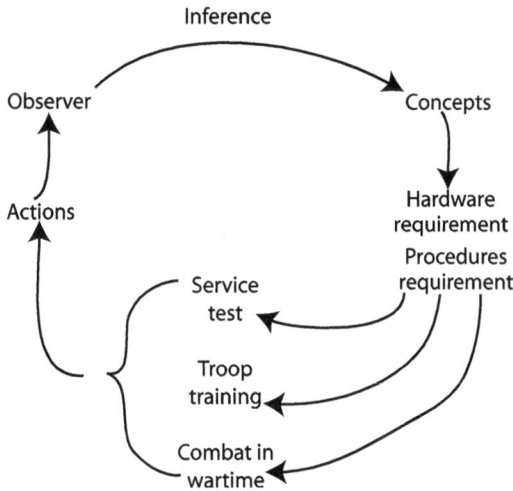

Figure 4. Formulation of Tactics and Techniques

First comes the *service test* during which a full-scale unit—a company, a squadron, a battery, or some other organization—puts the weapon through its paces. If this service test yields promising results, the new weapon is approved for production in quantity and issued to the troops in general. This brings us to the phase of routine troop training by operational units of the armed forces, involving individual and unit training, field exer-cises, and large-scale maneuvers. In addition, designated sup-port troops will receive specialized training in storing, issuing, maintaining, and repairing the new weapon. Each of these in phases affords opportunities for participants to observe and infer what needs doing to improve or advance the formulation of tactics and technique. Finally, in the event of war, the weapon is employed in actual combat, which stimulates even greater interest, not only in improving the hardware but also in perfecting the tactics and technique or doctrine being employed.

Observe how the two cycles interact: The hardware cycle with its implicit demand for suitable tactics and techniques for using and maintaining the weapon and the procedural cycle with its service testing, which determines whether a weapon is ready to put into mass production in the hardware cycle. Modifications in design that occur in the hardware cycle may well impose the necessity of changes in the doctrine devised in the procedural cycle. When John Browning developed his light, single-barrel machine-gun in 1890—a rapid-fire weapon at last which could be man-handled, the way was opened for a significant shift not only in organization but tactics; whereas Dr. Gatling's ponderous eight-barrel gun had been treated as an artillery piece, now at last the machine-gun was seen as an infantry weapon.

When one stands back and looks at the whole process in a detached way, it is evident that the crucial point in each cycle is the observer. Thousands of individuals may observe the new hardware or the new tactics, but only those who draw creative inferences from their observations keep the cycle moving. The individual who makes an inferential leap and comes up with a new concept is the creative soul the military services most desperately need.

Looking back from today's perspective, one can readily see that the nation dallied for more than 50 years before exploiting the machine-gun effectively. This delay came about, first, because the military authorities had failed to analyze the process, to see clearly the interacting hardware and procedural cycles. And, second, the authorities failed to develop a clear understanding of just how diverse concepts are distilled into doctrine. Nor did they always seem to appreciate that better doctrine helps attain better performance—more killing power, more effectiveness—out of existing weapons.

We may criticize the federal government or the Union Army for trying to increase its firepower by dragooning two-and-a-half million men into the ranks while all but ignoring the problem of doctrine. However, will we be any less open to criticism if we develop a superb aircraft—a complex weapon system, such as the B-1 at more than 60 million dollars a copy—and then fail to maximize our investment by some shortfall in our employment of that weapon and all its ancillary systems because we neglected to perfect an adequately tuned process for developing suitable doctrines, tactics, and techniques for employing them in combat with the enemy?

To illustrate the problem, we need only consider the example of a single service. What is Air Force doctrine today and how is it contrived? The place to begin is with the official definition. Unfortunately, this authoritative definition leaves something to be desired. The 1968 edition of the Joint Chiefs of Staff (JCS) *Dictionary of US Military Terms for Joint Usage* defined doctrine as "fundamental principles by which the military forces or elements thereof guide their actions in support of national objectives."[4] This definition had the virtue of being concise, but it was flawed in assuming that principles and doctrines are interchangeable terms, which they are not. There is another sentence in the definition, a sort of "Catch-22." Doctrine, as the 1968 JCS dictionary told us, is "authoritative but requires judgment in application." In other words, here are the generalized rules for employment, here are some guidelines for coping with your problem, but don't assume you can follow them slavishly—mechanically—in every situation. Doctrine manuals are not cookbooks to be followed precisely in every detail; they are not laws compelling mandatory compliance; they are suggestions based on historical experience. Every decision maker has to decide for himself in a given context just how far he should be guided by the official doctrine.

Just because the definition quoted above was officially approved by the JCS, we have no assurance that it was the best or most useful. An earlier version of the dictionary dated 1948, defined doctrine as "a compilation of principles and policies, developed through experience or by theory, that represents the best available thought, and indicate or guide but do not bind in practice. Its purpose is to provide that understanding within a force which generates mutual confidence between the commander and his subordinates in order that timely and effective action will be taken by all concerned in the absence of instructions."[5] In many respects the older definition may be superior to the 1968 version. The phrase "developed through experience" brings out effectively the notion that doctrine is largely derived from a distillation of cumulated experience, generalizing the best practices observed. This is schematically represented in figure 5. Concepts or tentative ideas based on observations of actual experience that have proved to be useful or effective in practice are the grist which, generalized, are formally cast as doctrinal statements. When officially approved by duly constituted authority, these statements become official doctrine.

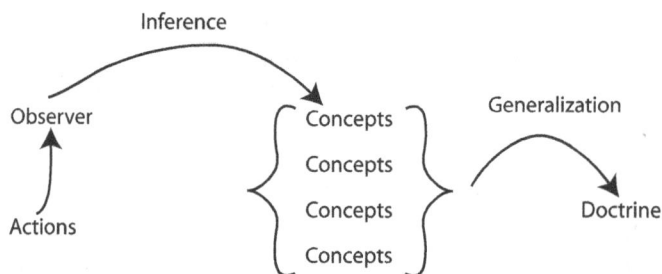

Figure 5. Doctrine Distillation Process

The older definition of doctrine has other virtues. It also gives recognition to the fact that sometimes in the absence of extended past experience, for example, with certain nuclear weapons, we must project or extrapolate doctrine on a largely theoretical basis. In any event, whichever definition one uses, doctrine is simply that which is authoritatively taught.

Each of the armed forces has an organization established to promulgate official doctrine, but in the final analysis doctrine really stems, ultimately, from the observations and inferences of perceptive individuals out where the action is. That brings the problem right back down to each and every individual in uniform, whatever his or her technical specialty or area of competence. Each must ask: What am I doing at my level of activity toward the development of usable doctrine? As the paradigm in figure 5 clearly shows, doctrine doesn't spring full-blown from the brow of prophets or seers on high in the Pentagon. Doctrine derives ultimately from the ideas and inferences, the concepts, of the individual observer at the grassroots.

The message of this essay should be obvious. It is not enough for the thoughtful individual to know what doctrine is and to understand the steps in its origins and how they interact. It's not enough merely to know how the doctrinal system functions. To be a truly responsible professional one must become involved in the process by contributing conceptual papers, engaging in debate to criticize, enhance, and perfect the concepts of others. What is needed, if doctrine is to be developed effectively, is a multitude of cases—examples from actual experience—that can be subjected to a critical and continuing dialogue, rigorously and objectively pursued.

William James, the philosopher of pragmatism, gives us a most useful point of departure when he points out that "all claims to truth must be publicly verifiable and meet the test of rival ideas in competition."[6] If one substitutes the term *sound doctrine* for *truth,* the implications become clear: what seems to be most notably lacking in the various organizations of the armed forces for devising doctrine is an adequate system for ensuring a continual flow of lively ideas—concepts—as candidates for doctrine and an adequate system for insuring that these rival ideas are pitted one against another in competition. There are too few fully effective "free market places of ideas" where concepts can be tested.

How many really cogent doctrinal studies can one find in the professional journals? How many challenging and controversial studies are to be found? There are some and a scattering of very good ones, but they are few and far between.[7] Where in the armed forces does one find a truly free and open forum where controversial ideas, novel and provocative concepts, and serious debunking of sacred cows take place? Do the armed forces actively encourage the publication of proposals and concept papers, even sober and solid studies, if they seriously challenge accepted practices and doctrines? Occasionally some bold individuals do launch such attempts and courageous editors publish them, but the practice has its dangers.

Here is what the editor of the US Naval Academy alumni magazine had to say when he addressed the problem of criticism from within the services: "The spirited and energetic support of a position which is not shared . . . by the commander has been known to make for a lively but foreshortened career. . . . [T]he spark of legitimate dissent is still too easily smothered. Not only does the system impress conformity, but also agreement is stressed to a point that substance itself may be sacrificed to the necessity of reaching agreed language. The written word is 'waffled' to accommodate divergent views in deliberate ambiguity."[8] One doesn't know whether these charges concerning the Navy are true or false. They are quoted only as a convenient, perhaps cowardly, way of too obviously stepping on the toes of the author's own service, the Air Forces. But to criticize the doctrines of a service, one must know what they are.

There used to be a regulation requiring all officers in the Air Force not only to have a copy of AF Manual 1-1, the basic doctrinal statement, but also to be familiar with its contents. That regulation was not one rigorously enforced. Perhaps there is some significance in the fate of that prescribed distribution for AFM 1-1, which called for one copy to every officer in the Air Force. The current revision has dropped back to a more modest allotment of one copy for every four officers. Should one conclude from this that the guardians of doctrine have given up trying to engage the minds of the whole officer corps and are willing to settle for the 25 percent who, they hope, will engage in serious thinking?

The prevailing level of interest or lack of interest in doctrine can be measured in other ways as well. Anyone checking that most useful bibliographic tool, the *Air University Library Index of Military Periodicals*, for the past 20 years under the heading "doctrine" will be dismayed at the slim pickings. The author conducted such a survey and discovered that in the decade between 1965 and 1975, both the Army and the Air Force averaged scarcely more than two or three articles a year on doctrine, this from the entire gamut of military journals published worldwide in the English language, some 60- or 70-odd titles in all. In the decade from 1975 to 1985, articles on Air Force doctrine averaged no more than three a year but those on Army doctrine had increased to an average of 10 each year. By way of contrast, an average of 10 Soviet articles on military doctrine were translated each year in the 1975–1985 decade, and this represents only a small part of total published in the many Soviet professional journals.

Of course, it is entirely possible that these skewed statistics indicate nothing more than some idiosyncrasy as to classification of titles on the part of the indexers. But one suspects they tell something important about the kind of thinking not being done often enough, at the very least, in the Air Force. Clearly what the services need is more officers and more scholars in academia who are willing to think about doctrine—and write about it to get their ideas into the market place. There is an unending requirement for original ideas that challenge long-accepted practices. There are literally hundreds of areas in the military sphere that cry out for innovative conceptual studies that can be used as the basis for perfecting doctrine. By no means all doctrinal issues relate to weaponry and combat. The need for doctrine is certainly no less pressing in the realm of support activities, in logistics and procurement, and in all the seemingly mundane problems of administration. A few examples should suffice.

There is a real need for thoughtful articles, doctrinal studies, in the personnel area. Consider, for example, the ever-recurring problem of a reduction-in-force (RIF) dictated by budget cuts. What harassed commander confronted with the always painful process of terminating civilian employees would not welcome a doctrinal manual reflecting the accumulated experience of others who have successfully navigated these treacherous waters? In this same area, how many officers who have spent years in military line units really understand how to relate effectively to the senior civil servants they encounter when assigned to a higher headquarters? Surely a doctrinal manual based on extensive study of the experience accrued by successful practitioners would serve a highly useful purpose.

For still other examples, consider these areas of activity for which soundly based doctrinal guidance are almost entirely lacking. Have any of the military services ever published an effective doctrine for dealing with the media? Learning to live with the press—and survive with reputation intact—is one of the more difficult challenges confronting officers who suddenly find themselves thrust into positions of high command where they are exposed to the merciless probing of investigative reporting, which is at once the bane and the glory of our great democracy. Or again, have any of the armed services perfected a doctrinal manual on Capitol Hill tactics? Year after year, high-ranking spokesmen, military and civilian, troop to the Hill to make the case for budgets and for implementing legislation. Some are notably more successful in this than others, but how much effort has been invested in winnowing out generalizable factors of their success for the instruction of newcomers? Must every newly appointed chief of staff or secretary learn the hard way? Must we assume that Hegel was not mistaken when he affirmed that "people and governments have never learned anything from history or acted on principles derived from it"?

Manifestly there is a continuing and urgent requirement for historically based studies that garner experience across the whole spectrum of military activities, from rifleman to accountant. But it is by no means enough to write and publish sound concept papers, valuable as such contributions can be. What is no less important is the resulting dialogue, the debate, the well-considered rejoinder in which the respondent raises objections and considerations that induce the promulgator of the original paper to rethink or revise or reinforce his original position. It is this dialectic process that develops truly valid generalizations that are the basis of sound doctrine.

Let me illustrate the importance of the dialectic by recalling a conversation with space pioneer Wernher von Braun in Huntsville, Alabama, not long before his death. He was talking about the alternate strategies being considered for an assault on the moon. One of the senior scientists, a distinguished individual at or near the top of the pecking order in the National Aeronautics and Space Administration (NASA), made a presentation on the proposed official mode of approach to the moon. He outlined an earth-orbit strategy in which the space ship would escape the earth's gravity and then orbit the earth, releasing a lunar lander, which would travel from there to the moon. All sorts of persuasive facts and figures were adduced to support the feasibility of this approach. It was an impressive performance.

There were, however, a couple of brash young scientists in the audience who proffered an alternative strategy. They proposed to escape the earth's gravitational field and take the space ship directly into orbit around the moon. From there they would dispatch the lunar lander to the surface of the moon. The senior scientist and his entourage made short work of the young men's proposal, pointing out all manner of flaws in their analysis. So the official bandwagon rolled on, and planning proceeded in terms of an earth-orbiting space ship.

But the young radicals persisted; they went back to their drawing boards and reworked their calculations to come out with a revised and improved proposal for a lunar-orbit strategy, only to be shot down again by older and wiser senior officials. This cycle was repeated several times with much the same result. Eventually, as everyone now knows, the course advocated by the young men won out. Their concept of a lunar orbit became the official choice, and that was the way the conquest of the moon was accomplished.

What are we to make of this tale? On the surface it looks like just another example of age and rank—the Establishment—stifling the brash but crucially important ideas of young challengers. One might draw this conclusion, but that is not what von Braun concluded from the episode. He pointed out that we owe a substantial debt to those senior scientists who advanced what turned out to be the road not taken. They didn't pull rank and brush off the young radicals; they respected their ideas even if they were inadequately supported in their initial presentations. These senior scientists saw the young men as worthy adversaries and engaged them in serious debate, taking the time to analyze their proposal and identify its flaws, its weaknesses, sending the young men back to their computers for another try.

When confronted with sustained, thoughtful opposition, the young men were forced to perfect their proposal by progressive steps until what had originally been a flawed and unworkable idea, unacceptable to the Establishment, at last became the official strategy for going to the moon. Would the resounding success of the subsequent moon flight have been possible, von Braun asked, without the sustained scientific dialogue that took place? No doubt the debate that took place in NASA flourished because that is the customary practice of scientists. Because military organizations are hierarchical and authoritarian, it may prove more difficult to foster a comparable dialectic, but that does not mean that it can't be done.

The point is not who is, in the final analysis, right or wrong, but how much and in what way each participant in the dialogue helps to advance our understanding of the problem. The objective of the dialectic is not to dominate but to illuminate issues as fully as possible, uncovering hitherto unrecognized dimensions and nuances. When it comes to validating ideas, two stars do not automatically outrank two bars. As Secretary of Defense James Schlesinger used to say, every man is entitled to his own opinion, but he's not entitled to his own set of facts. Fostering the dialectic is one of the more important tasks confronting the military services. Spending billions to perfect the hardware of weaponry while scanting the doctrines needed to exploit such hardware effectively makes little sense.

Contrary to popular understanding, our contemporaries in the Soviet armed forces not only understand the need for active debate as a prelude to the promulgation of sound doctrine but also actively encourage it in their numerous professional military journals. Perhaps nowhere is this more pointedly expressed than in a Russian military study by two Soviet officers, Druzhinin and Rontorov, entitled, in the official Air Force translation, *Concept, Algorithm, Decision*, "development . . . is possible only in the presence of contradictions. The absence of contradictions signifies . . . stagnation. The detection and disclosure of contradictions is the discovery of causes that give rise to progress."[9] We can neglect or ignore this message only at our peril.

Notes

1. Russell F. Weigley, *History of the US Army* (New York: Macmillan, 1967), 216.

2. For this and the successive paragraphs on the development of the machine-gun, see David A. Armstrong, *Bullets and Bureaucrats: The Machine-Gun and the US Army, 1861–1916* (Westport, Conn.: Greenwood Press, 1982), chapters 2, 3, and 5. See also Dominick Graham, "The British Expe-

ditionary Force in 1914 and the Machine-Gun," *Military Affairs* 46 (December 1982): 190–92.

3. The author saw the musket with unfired charges on display in a national park museum, a poignant reminder of the stress of battle and its impact on the individual infantryman.

4. Joint Chiefs of Staff, JCS Publication (JCS Pub) 1, *Dictionary of US Military Terms for Joint Usage* (Washington, D.C.: Government Printing Office [GPO], 1968).

5. JCS Pub 1, 1948 edition.

6. William James, *Pragmatism* (New York: Longmans, Green and Co., 1907).

7. For a representative sample, see the bibliographical essay, "Further Readings on Doctrine," at the end of this volume.

8. Capt Paul B. Schratz, "The American Tradition of Dissent" in Sea Breezes, *Shipmate* 38 (October 1975): 7.

9. V. V. Druzhinin and D. S. Rontorov, *Concept, Algorithm, Decision,* trans. and published, US Air Force (Washington, D.C.: GPO, 1975).

THIS PAGE INTENTIONALLY LEFT BLANK

Further Readings on Doctrine

Although the literature on doctrine and the processes by which military doctrine is evolved is not large, many books and articles will extend the interested reader's grasp of the subject substantially. More than the other services in the United States the Army has stimulated a good deal of writing on doctrine itself in specific applications and on the method by which doctrine is perfected. The professional military journals have, as one might expect, provided the principal forum for such discussions for many years.

John W. Taylor, "A Method for Developing Doctrine," *Military Review* 59 (March 1979): 70–75, and John C. Gazlay, "On Writing and Fighting: A Comparative Analysis of the Process," *Military Review* 58 (May 1978): 42–52, offer introductions to the method. For a brief history of the term *doctrine*, see Jay Luvaas, "Some Vagrant Thoughts on Doctrine," *Military Review* 66 (March 1986): 56–60. For an Army chief of staff's view of doctrine, see Gen George H. Decker, "Doctrine: the Cement That Binds," *Army* 11 (February 1961): 60. For a narrative account of how the Army doctrine of the 1980s emerged, see John L. Romjue, *From Active Defense to AirLand Battle: The Development of Army Doctrine, 1973–1982,* a volume published by the US Army Training and Doctrine Command, Fort Monroe, Va. (1984). Included in this item is a significant document by a leading Army doctrinal thinker, Gen Donn Starry, "Operational Concepts and Doctrine," *TRADOC Commander's Notes*, no. 3 (20 February 1979). For the historical background on air-ground relations, one should read Pegasus, "The Forty Year Split," a series of articles in *Army* 15 (July 1965): 46–51; (August 1965): 56–60; and (October 1965): 62–66.

Michael D. Krause, "Arthur Wagner: Doctrine and the Lessons from the Past," *Military Review* 58 (November 1978): 53–59, deals with a pioneer in doctrinal studies. An excellent case history can be found in David A. Armstrong, *Bullets and Bureaucrats: The Machine-Gun and the United States Army, 1861–1916* (Westport, Conn.: Greenwood Press, 1982).

For a survey of evolving Air Force doctrine, the essential study is Robert Frank Futrell, *Ideas, Concepts, Doctrine: A History of*

Basic Thinking in the US Air Force, 1907–1964 (Maxwell Air Force Base, Ala.: Air University, Aerospace Studies Institute, 1974). For a briefer treatment, see Futrell's "Some Patterns of Air Force Thought," *Air University Review* 15 (January 1964): 81–88. Also useful is Dale 0. Smith, *US Military Doctrine: A Study and Appraisal* (New York: Duell, Sloan, and Pearce, 1955). See also I. B. Holley Jr., "An Enduring Challenge: The Problem of Air Force Doctrine," USAF Academy, Harmon Lecture no. 16, 1974.

For air doctrine in World War I see Malcom Cooper, "The Development of Air Policy and Doctrine on the Western Front, 1914–1918," *Aerospace Historian* 28 (Spring 1981): 38–51, and Thomas H. Greer, "Air Arm Doctrinal Roots, 1917–1918," *Military Affairs* 20 (Winter 1956): 202–16. More sweeping surveys are in James L. Cate, "Development of Air Arm Doctrine, 1917–1941," *Air University Quarterly Review* 1 (Winter 1947): 11–22; and Thomas H. Greer, *The Development of Army Air Doctrine in the Army Air Arm, 1917–1941* (Maxwell AFB, Ala.: Air University, USAF Historical Studies, 1955).

On the ever-challenging topic of close air support doctrine in World War II, two useful studies are William A. Jacobs, "Tactical Air Doctrine and AAF Close Air Support in the European Theater, 1944–1945," *Aerospace Historian* 27 (March 1950): 35–49; and Laurence S. Kuter, "Goddammit Georgie! North Africa, 1943: the birth of tactical air doctrine," *Air Force* 56 (February 1973): 51–6. Insights relating to the ongoing development of air doctrine will be found in Ken Pullen, "There is a Way—Inputs to Tactics Development," *Fighter Weapons Review* 34 (Spring 1986): 33–34.

For a critique of Air Force doctrinal thinking since World War II, see Dennis M. Drew, "Of Trees and Leaves: A New View of Doctrine," *Air University Review* 33 (January 1982): 40–48. On USAF space doctrine two useful articles are Dino Lorenzini, "Space Power Doctrine," *Air University Review* 33 (July 1982): 16–21; and L. Parkes Temple, "How Dare They Tamper With the Sacred Functions of the Horse Cavalry," *Air University Review* 37 (March 1986): 24–30.

An early essay on naval doctrine is Dudley W. Knox, "The Role of Doctrine in Naval Warfare," US Naval Institute *Proceedings* 41 (March 1915): 325–66. A brilliant and provocative article by a former Naval Academy faculty member is W. H. Russell, "Mahan's Doctrine and the Air Age," *Military Affairs* 20 (Winter 1956): 227–29. The Mahan theme is picked up also by George C. Reinhardt, "Air Power Needs a Mahan," US Naval Institute *Proceedings* 78 (April 1952): 363–67.

An excellent article on the relationship between maneuvers or exercises and the development of doctrine is Frederick Thompson, "Did We Learn Anything From That Exercize? Could We?" *Naval War College Review* 35 (July 1982): 25–37. On the relationship between research and development and doctrine in a naval context, see Thomas C. Hone and Mark D. Mandeles, "Interwar Innovation in Three Navies: US Navy, Royal Navy, Imperial Japanese Navy," *Naval War College Review* 40 (Spring 1987): 63–83. Insights on Marine Corps doctrine will be found in Richard S. Moore, "Ideas and Direction: Building Amphibious Doctrine," *Marine Corps Gazette* 66 (November 1982): 49–58.

On communications doctrine, Paul W. Clark gives the historical background in "Early Impacts of Communications on Doctrine," *IEEE Proceedings* 64 (September 1976): 407–13. Two more contemporary studies are W. E. Lotz, "Military Requirements and Technology," *Signal* 23 (October 1968): 42–45; and J. B. McKinney, "Doctrinal Revolution in Communications-Electronics," *Signal* 22 (April 1968): 38–41.

One of the very best studies of how doctrine is evolved is Timothy T. Lupfer, *The Dynamics of Doctrine: The Changes in German Tactical Doctrine during the First World War* (Fort Leavenworth, Kans.: US Army Combat Studies Institute, 1981). Also excellent on German doctrinal practices is Williamson Murray, "A Tale of Two Doctrines: The Luftwaffe's 'Conduct of the Air War' and the USAF's Manual 1–1," *Journal of Strategic Studies* 6 (December 1983): 84–93. Two useful studies of British experience with doctrine are W. H. E. Travers, "The Offensive and the Problem of Innovation in British Military Thought, 1870–1915," *Journal of Contemporary History* 13 (July 1978): 531–54; and Dominick Graham, "The British Expeditionary Force in 1914 and the Machine-Gun," *Military Affairs* 46 (December 1982): 190–92. An outstanding study on French military doctrine is Robert A. Doughty, *The Seeds of*

Disaster: The Development of French Army Doctrine, 1919–1939 (Hamden, Conn.: Archon Books, 1985). See also Doughty's "The Enigma of French Armored Doctrine, 1940," *Armor* (September 1974), 39–44; and Harold R. Winton, *To Change An Army: General Sir John Burnett Stuart and British Armored Doctrine* (Lawrence, Kans.: University Press of Kansas, 1988). An important caveat on the difficulties of converting "experience" into a "lesson" and the dangers of doctrine becoming dogma—master rather than servant—is to be found in the introduction to the second edition of Jay Luvaas, *The Military Legacy of the Civil War: The European Inheritance* (Lawrence, Kans.: University Press of Kansas, 1988), ix–xxx.

Especially useful for its insights on the need to question our assumptions concerning enemy capabilities is Gordon H. McCormick, "The Dynamics of Doctrinal Change," *Orbis* 27 (Summer 1983): 266–74. For the difficulties of equating advancing technology with doctrine, a helpful study is Kevin N. Lewis, "On the Appropriate Use of Technology," *Orbis* 37 (Summer 1983): 274–85. George C. Reinhardt offers a plea for nuclear doctrine in "The Doctrinal Gap", US Naval Institute *Proceedings* 92 (August 1966): 61–69. Finally, a highly provocative article on the need for imaginative thinking as a precondition to the formulation of doctrine is Oron P. South, "The Door to the Future: Understanding the Barriers to Creative Thinking," *Air University Quarterly Review* 9 (Winter 1957): 110–26.

The foregoing list is representative rather than exhaustive; though limited, it should serve as an introduction to the many ramifications of military doctrine.

Technology and Military Doctrine
Essays on a Challenging Relationship

Air University Press Team

Chief Editor
Thomas C. Lobenstein

Copy Editor
Carolyn J. McCormack

Cover Art and Book Design
L. Susan Fair

*Composition and
Prepress Production*
Mary P. Ferguson

Print Preparation
Joan Hickey

Distribution
Diane Clark

www.ingramcontent.com/pod-product-compliance
Lightning Source LLC
Chambersburg PA
CBHW080017280326
41934CB00015B/3374